After Gettysburg

Lee retreats, Meade pursues

Editor: Joe Mieczkowski, Licensed Battlefield Guide, Gettysburg NMP

Title: After Gettysburg

Subtitle: Lee retreats, Meade pursues

Editor: Joe Mieczkowski, Licensed Battlefield Guide, Gettysburg NMP

Created on: 2016-09-26 08:22 (UTC)

ISBN: 978-3-86898-009-7

Produced by: PediaPress GmbH, Moritz-Hilf-Str. 26, Limburg an der Lahn, Germany, http://pediapress.com/

Create your own custom Wikipedia-Book at http://pediapress.com

collection id:
pdf writer version: 0.10.4 mwlib version: 0.15.18

Contents

Leadership after Gettysburg: Lee retreats and Meade pursues

At the close of the Battle of Gettysburg on July 3, 1863, the Army of the Potomac, led by Maj. Gen. George Gordon Meade had won the Union's first indisputable victory in the East. After the battle, Lee was able to retreat back into Virginia.

With Gettysburg's effect magnified by news of Grant's capture of Vicksburg, Miss., on July 4, the Confederacy was left with no realistic chance of winning the war militarily. The Confederate government in Richmond could only hope for a political settlement.

Terrified just days before, Washington responded to Meade's stunning victory by criticizing him for not destroying Lee's army — an army with plenty of fight left in it, as the next two years would show. The gratitude of politicians was as slight then as it is now. On July 14, 1863 President Abraham Lincoln wrote, but never sent, a letter to General George G. Meade following Robert E. Lee's retreat from Gettysburg. The letter read, "Again, my dear general, I do not believe you appreciate the magnitude of the misfortune involved in Lee's escape. He was within your easy grasp, and to have closed upon him would, in connection with our other late successes, have ended the war. As it is, the war will be prolonged indefinitely."

Ending the war, however, was very much on the mind of The Commanding General of the Army of the Potomac as he pursued and attempted to close upon Lee during the remainder of the year. Meade organized a pursuit of Lee as quickly as he could, slowed by his own severe losses, the tens of thousands of wounded left on the field, and troops who were out of food and ammunition. He had just done the impossible and was damned for not doing the impossible twice in a row.

Meade continued to command his army during the Bristoe Station and Mine Run campaigns, but both proved to be indecisive. And yet Meade did not lose the Battle of Gettysburg—if he had, the results would have been catastrophic for the Union, even with the offset of the fall of Vicksburg on July 4. But he allowed his own instinct for risk aversion to keep him from turning it into a crushing victory.

In the fall of 1863 the Confederacy used their interior lines of communication to transfer two divisions and an artillery battalion of Lieutenant General James Longstreet's I Corps, Army of Northern Virginia, by railroad from Virginia to Georgia to reinforce General Braxton Bragg's Army of Tennessee. The troops began arriving at the Catoosa Platform, Georgia on September 19, having begun their journey from Virginia on September 9, ultimately only 5 of Longstreet's 10 infantry brigades arrived in time to participate in the Confederate victory at Chickamauga.

Following their defeat, the troops of Major General William Rosecrans' Army of the Cumberland fell back to Chattanooga, Tennessee where they were surrounded by the Confederates who occupied the heights surrounding the town. On the evening of September 23, 1863, Secretary of War Edwin Stanton convened a meeting with President Lincoln, Major General Henry Halleck, Secretary of State William Seward and Treasury Secretary Salmon Chase to review plans to reinforce and relieve the Army of the Cumberland with troops from other Union departments.

Major General George Meade, the commander of the Army of the Potomac, was directed to prepare the XI and XII Corps for movement beginning September 25. At the time the XII Corps' two divisions were on picket duty along the Rappahannock River and had to be relieved by the I Corps before it could move to the railroad. The XI Corps' remaining two divisions were deployed to the army's rear guarding the Orange and Alexandria. Meade initially ordered the XII Corps to march to Brandy Station, but the corps was directed to march 10 miles further up the railroad to Bealeton where there were better arrangements for loading the trains. The XI Corps infantry moved to Manassas Junction, Virginia to board trains.

By October 12, the USMRR and civilian railroads completed the movement of both corps to participate in the fighting to relieve the Army of the Cumberland at Chattanooga.

From November 27 to December 3, 1863, Confederate troops under General James Longstreet lay siege to the city of Knoxville held by Union forces under General Ambrose Burnside. Longstreet attacks on November 30 but is repulsed with heavy losses. The arrival of Union reinforcements forces him to withdraw to Greeneville, Tennessee, where his corps will spend the winter.

In the spring of 1864, Ulysses S. Grant, the newly appointed lieutenant general and general-in-chief of Union forces, made his headquarters with the Army of the Potomac. Although Meade was nominally in charge of the Army of the Potomac, Grant made all command decisions in regards to the movement of the army. Still, Meade would be the only commander of the Army of the Potomac never dismissed. He would serve until the last victory. Those who mattered knew his worth.

The Battle of Gettysburg was a major defeat for the South. Lee's army, dangerous as it was until the very last, would never again have the punch — in numbers, morale, quality and quantity of officers — that it took into Pennsylvania in June 1863. Whether or not Meade could have made the wound he had inflicted a mortal one remains one of the great unanswerable questions of the war. This book pulls together the significant battles in the East after Gettysburg in 1863 and fills a void in Civil War literature in an attempt to answer those questions.

The biographies of noteworthy individuals after Gettysburg are included: William H. French, John Imboden, William E. Jones, Judson Kilpatrick, John Sedgwick, JEB Stuart and Gouverneur K. Warren.

Joe Mieczkowski is a Licensed Battlefield Guide at The Gettysburg National Military Park. He retired from the Federal Government following 38 years of service. Mieczkowski is a faculty member of The Lincoln Leadership Institute in Gettysburg, Pennsylvania. He is the past President of The Association of Licensed Battlefield Guides and of The Gettysburg Civil War Roundtable. He has two books to his credit, Lincoln and his Cabinet and Jefferson Davis and his Cabinet.

Lee Retreats

Retreat from Gettysburg

The Confederate Army of Northern Virginia began its **Retreat from Gettysburg** on July 4, 1863. Following General Robert E. Lee's failure to defeat the Union Army at the Battle of Gettysburg (July 1–3, 1863), he ordered a retreat through Maryland and over the Potomac River to relative safety in Virginia. The Union Army of the Potomac, commanded by Maj. Gen. George G. Meade, was unable to maneuver quickly enough to launch a significant attack on the Confederates, who crossed the river on the night of July 13–14.

Confederate supplies and thousands of wounded men proceeded over South Mountain through Cashtown in a wagon train that extended for 15–20 miles, enduring harsh weather, treacherous roads, and enemy cavalry raids. The bulk of Lee's infantry departed through Fairfield and through the Monterey Pass toward Hagerstown, Maryland. Reaching the Potomac, they found that rising waters and destroyed pontoon bridges prevented their immediate crossing. Erecting substantial defensive works, they awaited the arrival of the Union army, which had been pursuing over longer roads more to the south of Lee's route. Before Meade could perform adequate reconnaissance and attack the Confederate fortifications, Lee's army escaped across fords and a hastily rebuilt bridge.

Combat operations, primarily cavalry battles, raids, and skirmishes, occurred during the retreat at Fairfield (July 3), Monterey Pass (July 4–5), Smithsburg (July 5), Hagerstown (July 6 and 12), Boonsboro (July 8), Funkstown (July 7 and 10), and around Williamsport and Falling Waters (July 6–14). Additional clashes after the armies crossed the Potomac occurred at Shepherdstown (July 16) and Manassas Gap (July 23) in Virginia, ending the Gettysburg Campaign of June and July 1863.

Figure 1: *Commanding generals Meade and Lee.*

Background

Military situation

The culmination of the three-day Battle of Gettysburg was the massive infantry assault known as Pickett's Charge, in which the Confederate attack against the center of the Union line on Cemetery Ridge was repulsed with significant losses. The Confederates returned to their positions on Seminary Ridge and prepared to receive a counterattack. When the Union attack had not occurred by the evening of July 4, Lee realized that he could accomplish nothing more in his Gettysburg Campaign and that he had to return his battered army to Virginia. His ability to supply his army by living off the Pennsylvania countryside was now significantly reduced and the Union could easily bring up additional reinforcements as time passed, whereas he could not. Brig. Gen. William N. Pendleton, Lee's artillery chief, reported to him that all of his long-range artillery ammunition had been expended and there were no early prospects for resupply. However, despite casualties of over 20,000 officers and men, including a number of senior officers, the morale of Lee's army remained high and their respect for the commanding general was not diminished by their reverses.[1]

Lee began his preparations for retreat on the night of July 3, following a council of war with some of his subordinate commanders. He consolidated his lines by pulling Lt. Gen. Richard S. Ewell's Second Corps from the Culp's Hill area back through the town of Gettysburg and onto Oak Ridge and Seminary Ridge. His men constructed breastworks and rifle pits that extended 2.5 miles from the Mummasburg Road to the Emmitsburg Road. He decided to send his long train of wagons carrying equipment and supplies, which had been captured in great quantities throughout the campaign, to the rear as quickly as possible, in advance of the infantry. The wagon train included ambulances with his 8,000 wounded men[2] who were fit to travel, as well as some of the key general officers who were severely wounded, but too important to be abandoned. The great bulk of the Confederate wounded—over 6,800 men—remained behind to be treated in Union field hospitals and by a few of Lee's surgeons selected to stay with them.[3]

There were two routes the army could take over South Mountain to the Cumberland Valley (the name given to the Shenandoah Valley in Maryland and Pennsylvania), from where it would march south to cross the Potomac at Williamsport, Maryland: the Chambersburg Pike, which passed through Cashtown in the direction of Chambersburg, and; the shorter route through Fairfield and over Monterey Pass to Hagerstown. Fortunately for the Confederate army, it now had its full complement of cavalry available for reconnaissance and screening activities, a capability it lacked earlier in the campaign while its commander, Maj. Gen. J.E.B. Stuart, was separated from the army with his three best cavalry brigades on "Stuart's ride".[4]

Unfortunately for the Confederate Army, however, once they reached the Potomac they would find it difficult to cross. Torrential rains that started on July 4 flooded the river at Williamsport, making fording impossible. Four miles downstream at Falling Waters, Union cavalry dispatched from Harpers Ferry by Maj. Gen. William H. French destroyed Lee's lightly guarded pontoon bridge on July 4. The only way to cross the river was a small ferry at Williamsport. The Confederates could potentially be trapped, forced to defend themselves against Meade with their backs to the river.[5]

Opposing forces

The Union Army of the Potomac and the Confederate Army of Northern Virginia retained their general organizations with which they fought at the Battle of Gettysburg. By July 10, some of the Union battle losses had been replaced and Meade's Army stood at about 80,000 men. The Confederates received no reinforcements during the campaign and had only about 50,000 men available.[6]

Union

The **Army of the Potomac** had significant changes in general officer assignments because of its battle losses. Meade's chief of staff, Maj. Gen. Daniel Butterfield, was wounded on July 3 and was replaced on July 8 by Maj. Gen. Andrew A. Humphreys; Brig. Gen. Henry Price replaced Humphreys in command of his old division of the III Corps. Maj. Gen. John F. Reynolds, killed on July 1, was replaced by Maj. Gen. John Newton of the VI Corps. Maj. Gen. Winfield S. Hancock of the II Corps, wounded on July 3, was replaced by Brig. Gen. William Hays. Maj. Gen. William H. French, who had temporarily commanded the garrison at Harpers Ferry for most of the campaign, replaced the wounded Daniel E. Sickles in command of the III Corps on July 7. In addition to the battle losses, Meade's army was plagued by a condition that persisted during the war, the departure of men and regiments whose enlistments had expired, which took effect even in the midst of an active campaign. On the plus side, however, Meade had available temporary, although inexperienced, reinforcements of about 10,000 men who had been with General French at Maryland Heights, which were incorporated into the I Corps and III Corps. The net effect of expiring enlistments and reinforcements added about 6,000 men to the Army of the Potomac. Including the forces around Harpers Ferry, Maryland Heights, and the South Mountain passes, by July 14 between 11,000 and 12,000 men had been added the army, although Meade had extreme doubts about the combat effectiveness of these troops. In addition to the Army of the Potomac, Maj. Gen. Darius N. Couch of the Department of the Susquehanna had 7,600 men at Waynesboro, 11,000 at Chambersburg, and 6,700 at Mercersburg. These were "emergency troops" that were hastily raised during Lee's march into Pennsylvania and were subject to Meade's orders.[7] In addition, a force of about 6,000 from the newly created Department of West Virginia under Brig. Gen. Benjamin Franklin Kelley sat astride the Baltimore & Ohio Railroad at Grafton, and New Creek, to prevent Confederate forces from retreating west, as well as later assisting in the pursuit of Lee toward Virginia.[8]

Confederate

Lee's **Army of Northern Virginia** retained its corps organization and commanders, although a number of key subordinate generals were killed (Lewis A. Armistead, Richard B. Garnett, Isaac E. Avery), captured (James L. Kemper and James J. Archer), or severely wounded (John B. Hood, Wade Hampton, George T. Anderson, Dorsey Pender, and Alfred M. Scales).[9]

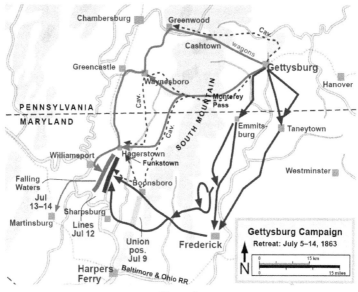

Figure 2:
Gettysburg Campaign (July 5–14)
Confederate
Union

Imboden's wagon train

At 1 a.m. on July 4, Lee summoned to his headquarters Brig. Gen. John D. Imboden, one of Stuart's cavalry brigade commanders, to manage the passage of the majority of the trains to the rear. Imboden's command of 2,100 cavalrymen had not played much of a role in the campaign up until this time, and had not been selected by Stuart for his ride around the Union Army. Lee and Stuart had a poor opinion of Imboden's brigade, considering it "indifferently disciplined and inefficiently directed," but it was effective for assignments such as guard duty or fighting militia. Lee reinforced Imboden's single artillery battery with five additional batteries borrowed from his infantry corps and directed Stuart to assign the brigades of Brig. Gen. Fitzhugh Lee and Wade Hampton (now commanded by Col. Laurence S. Baker) to protect the flanks and rear of Imboden's column. Imboden's orders were to depart Cashtown on the evening of July 4, turn south at Greenwood, avoiding Chambersburg, take the direct road to Williamsport to ford across the Potomac, and escort the train as far as Martinsburg. Then, Imboden's command would return to Hagerstown to guard the retreat route for the remainder of the army.[10]

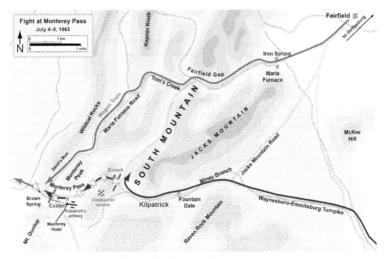

Figure 3: *Fight at Monterey Pass*

Imboden's train consisted of hundreds of Conestoga-style wagons, which extended 15–20 miles along the narrow roads. Assembling these wagons into a marching column, arranging their escorts, loading supplies, and accounting for the wounded took until late afternoon on July 5. Imboden himself left Cashtown around 8 p.m. to join the head of his column. The journey was one of extreme misery, conducted during the torrential rains that began on July 4, in which the wounded men were forced to endure the weather and the rough roads in wagons without suspensions. Imboden's orders required that he not stop until he reached his destination, which meant that wagons breaking down were left behind. Some critically wounded men were left behind on the roadsides as well, hoping that local civilians would find and take care of them. The train was harassed throughout its march. At dawn on July 5, civilians in Greencastle ambushed the train with axes, attacking the wheels of the wagons, until they were driven off. That afternoon at Cunningham's Cross Roads (current day Cearfoss, Maryland), Capt. Abram Jones led 200 troopers of the 1st New York Cavalry and 12th Pennsylvania Cavalry in attacking the column, capturing 134 wagons, 600 horses and mules, and 645 prisoners, about half of whom were wounded. These losses so angered Stuart that he demanded a court of inquiry to investigate.[11]

Fairfield and Monterey Pass

After dark on July 4, Hill's Third Corps headed out onto the Fairfield Road, followed by Lt. Gen. James Longstreet's First Corps and Richard S. Ewell's

Second Corps. Lee accompanied Hill at the head of the column. He ordered Stuart to post Col. John R. Chambliss's and Brig. Gen. Albert G. Jenkins's brigades (the latter commanded by Col. Milton Ferguson) to cover his left rear from Emmitsburg. Departing in the dark, Lee had the advantage of getting several hours head start and the route from the west side of the battlefield to Williamsport was about half as long as the ones available to the Army of the Potomac.[12]

Meade was reluctant to begin an immediate pursuit because he was unsure whether Lee intended to attack again and his orders continued that he was required to protect the cities of Baltimore and Washington, D.C. Since Meade believed that the Confederates had well fortified the South Mountain passes, he decided he would pursue Lee on the east side of the mountains, conduct forced marches to quickly seize the passes west of Frederick, Maryland, and threaten Lee's left flank as he retreated up the Cumberland Valley. However, Meade's assumption was wrong—Fairfield was lightly held by only two small cavalry brigades and the passes over South Mountain were not fortified. If Meade had secured Fairfield, Lee's army would have been forced to either fight its way through Fairfield while its rear was exposed to the Army of the Potomac at Gettysburg or to take his entire army through the Cashtown Pass, a much more difficult route to Hagerstown.[13]

On July 3, while Pickett's Charge was underway, the Union cavalry had had a unique opportunity to impede Lee's eventual retreat. Brig. Gen. Wesley Merritt's brigade departed from Emmitsburg with orders from cavalry commander Maj. Gen. Alfred Pleasonton to strike the Confederate right and rear along Seminary Ridge. Reacting to a report from a local civilian that there was a Confederate forage train near Fairfield, Merritt dispatched about 400 men in four squadrons from the 6th U.S. Cavalry under Major Samuel H. Starr to seize the wagons. Before they were able to reach the wagons, the 7th Virginia Cavalry, leading a column under Confederate Brig. Gen. William E. "Grumble" Jones, intercepted the regulars, starting the minor Battle of Fairfield. Taking cover behind a post-and rail fence, the U.S. cavalrymen opened fire and caused the Virginians to retreat. Jones sent in the 6th Virginia Cavalry, which successfully charged and swarmed over the Union troopers, wounding and capturing Starr. There were 242 Union casualties, primarily prisoners, and 44 casualties among the Confederates. Despite the relatively small scale of this action, its result was that the strategically important Fairfield Road to the South Mountain passes remained open.[14]

Early on July 4 Meade sent his cavalry to strike the enemy's rear and lines of communication so as to "harass and annoy him as much as possible in his retreat." Eight of nine cavalry brigades (except Col. John B. McIntosh's of Brig. Gen. David McM. Gregg's division) took to the field. Col. J. Irvin Gregg's brigade (of his cousin David Gregg's division) moved toward Cashtown via Hunterstown and the Mummasburg Road, but all of the others moved south of Gettysburg. Brig. Gen. John Buford's division went directly from Westminster to Frederick, where they were joined by Merritt's division on the night of July 5.[15]

Late on July 4, Meade held a council of war in which his corps commanders agreed that the army should remain at Gettysburg until Lee acted, and that the cavalry should pursue Lee in any retreat. Meade decided to have Brig. Gen. Gouverneur K. Warren take a division from Maj. Gen. John Sedgwick's VI Corps—the most lightly engaged of all the Union corps at Gettysburg—to probe the Confederate line and determine Lee's intentions. Meade ordered Butterfield to prepare for a general movement of the army, which he organized into three wings, commanded by Sedgwick (I, III, and VI Corps), Maj. Gen. Henry W. Slocum (II and XII), and Maj. Gen. Oliver O. Howard (V and XI). By the morning of July 5, Meade learned of Lee's departure, but he hesitated to order a general pursuit until he had received the results of Warren's reconnaissance.[16]

The Battle of Monterey Pass began as Brig. Gen. Judson Kilpatrick's cavalry division arrived near Fairfield on July 4 just before dark. They easily brushed aside Brig. Gen. Beverly Robertson's pickets and encountered a detachment of 20 men from the Confederate 1st Maryland Cavalry Battalion, under Capt. G. M. Emack, that was guarding the road to Monterey Pass. Aided by a detachment of the 4th North Carolina Cavalry and a single cannon, the Marylanders delayed the advance of 4,500 Union cavalrymen until well after midnight. Kilpatrick was not able to see anything in the dark and considered his command to be in "a perilous situation." He ordered Brig. Gen. George A. Custer to charge the Confederates with the 6th Michigan Cavalry, which broke the deadlock and allowed Kilpatrick's men to reach and attack the wagon train. They captured or destroyed numerous wagons and captured 1,360 prisoners—primarily wounded men in ambulances—and a large number of horses and mules.[17]

Following the fight at Monterey, Kilpatrick's division reached Smithsburg around 2 p.m. on July 5. Stuart arrived from over South Mountain with the brigades of Chambliss and Ferguson. A horse artillery duel ensued, causing some damage to the small town. Kilpatrick withdrew at dark "to save my prisoners, animals, and wagons" and arrived at Boonsboro (spelled Boonsborough at that time) before midnight.[18]

Sedgwick's reconnaissance

The reconnaissance from Sedgwick's corps began before dawn on the morning of July 5, but instead of a division they took the entire corps. It struck the rear guard of Ewell's corps late in the afternoon at Granite Hill near Fairfield, but the result was little more than a skirmish, and the Confederates camped a mile and a half west of Fairfield, holding their position with only their picket line. Warren informed Meade that he and Sedgwick believed Lee was concentrating the main body of his army around Fairfield and preparing for battle. Meade immediately halted his army and early on the morning of July 6, he ordered Sedgwick to resume his reconnaissance to determine Lee's intentions and the status of the mountain passes. Sedgwick argued with him about the risky nature of sending his entire corps into the rugged country and dense fog ahead of him and by noon Meade abandoned his plan, resuming his original intention of advancing east of the mountains to Middletown, Maryland. The delays leaving Gettysburg and the conflicting orders to Sedgwick about whether to conduct merely a reconnaissance or a vigorous advance to engage Lee's army in combat would later cause Meade political difficulties as his opponents charged him with indecision and timidity.[19]

Edwin B. Coddington, *The Gettysburg Campaign*[20]

Given the conflicting signals from Meade, Sedgwick and Warren followed the more conservative course. They waited to start until Ewell's Corps had cleared out of Fairfield and remained at a safe distance behind it as it moved west. Lee assumed that Sedgwick would attack his rear and was ready for it. He told Ewell, "If these people keep coming on, turn back and thresh them." Ewell replied, "By the blessing of Providence I will do it" and ordered Maj. Gen. Robert E. Rodes's division to form a battle line. The VI Corps followed Lee only to the top of Monterey Pass, however, and did not pursue down the other side.[21]

Pursuit to Williamsport

Ted Alexander, *Washington Times*[22]

Before Meade's infantry began to march in earnest in pursuit of Lee, Buford's cavalry division departed from Frederick to destroy Imboden's train before it could cross the Potomac. Hagerstown was a key point on the Confederate retreat route, and seizing it might block or delay their access to the fords across the river. On July 6, Kilpatrick's division, after its success raiding at Monterey Pass, moved toward Hagerstown and pushed out the two small brigades of Chambliss and Robertson. However, infantry commanded by Brig. Gen. Alfred Iverson drove Kilpatrick's men back through the streets of town. Stuart's

INVASION OF MARYLAND—GENERAL MEADE'S ARMY CROSSING THE ANTIETAM IN PURSUIT OF LEE, JULY 12 —FROM A SKETCH BY
OUR SPECIAL ARTIST, E. FORBES.

Figure 4: *Invasion of Maryland - General Meade's army
crossing the Antietam in pursuit of Lee, July 12, engrav-
ing for Frank Leslie's illustrated newspaper by Edwin Forbes.*

remaining brigades came up and were reinforced by two brigades of Hood's
Division and Hagerstown was recaptured by the Confederates.[23]

Buford heard Kilpatrick's artillery in the vicinity and requested support on his
right. Kilpatrick chose to respond to Buford's request for assistance and join
the attack on Imboden at Williamsport. Stuart's men pressured Kilpatrick's
rear and right flank from their position at Hagerstown and Kilpatrick's men
gave way and exposed Buford's rear to the attack. Buford gave up his effort
when darkness fell. At 5 p.m. on July 7 Buford's men reached within a half-
mile of the parked trains, but Imboden's command repulsed their advance.[24]

The Battle of Boonsboro occurred along the National Road on July 8. Stuart advanced from the direction of Funkstown and Williamsport with five
brigades. He first encountered Union resistance at Beaver Creek Bridge, 4.5
miles north of Boonsboro. By 11 a.m., the Confederate cavalry had pushed
forward to several mud-soaked fields, where fighting on horseback was nearly
impossible, forcing Stuart's troopers and Kilpatrick's and Buford's divisions to
fight dismounted. By mid-afternoon, the Union left under Kilpatrick crumbled
as the Federals ran low on ammunition under increasing Confederate pressure.
Stuart's advance ended about 7 p.m., however, when Union infantry arrived,
and Stuart withdrew north to Funkstown.[25]

Figure 5: *Earthworks in Lee's Potomac line (Last stand of the Army of Virginia, commanded by General Lee), painting by Edwin Forbes.*

Stuart's strong presence at Funkstown threatened any Union advance toward Williamsport, posing a serious risk to the Federal right and rear if the Union army moved west from Boonsboro. As Buford's division cautiously approached Funkstown via the National Road on July 10, it encountered Stuart's crescent-shaped, three-mile-long battle line, initiating the [Second] Battle of Funkstown (the first being a minor skirmish on July 7 between Buford's 6th U.S. Cavalry and the 7th Virginia Cavalry of Grumble Jones's brigade), Col. Thomas C. Devin's dismounted Union cavalry brigade attacked about 8 a.m. By mid-afternoon, with Buford's cavalrymen running low on ammunition and gaining little ground, Col. Lewis A. Grant's First Vermont Brigade of infantry arrived and clashed with Brig. Gen. George T. Anderson's Confederate brigade (commanded after Anderson's wounding at Gettysburg by Col. William W. White), the first time opposing infantry had fought since the Battle of Gettysburg. By early evening, Buford's command began withdrawing south towards Beaver Creek, where the Union I, VI, and XI Corps had concentrated.[26]

Buford and Kilpatrick continued to hold their advance position around Boonsboro, awaiting the arrival of the Army of the Potomac. French's command sent troops to destroy the railroad bridge at Harpers Ferry and a brigade to occupied Maryland Heights, which prevented the Confederates from outflanking the lower end of South Mountain and threatening Frederick from the southwest.[27]

Face-off at the Potomac

Meade's infantry had been marching hard since the morning of July 7. Slocum's wing marched 29 miles on the first day from Littlestown, Pennsylvania, to Walkersville, Maryland. Parts of the XI Corps covered distances estimated between 30 and 34 miles from Emmitsburg to Middletown. By July 9 most of the Army of the Potomac was concentrated in a 5-mile line from Rohrersville to Boonsboro. Other Union forces were in position to protect the outer flanks at Maryland Heights and at Waynesboro. Reaching these positions was difficult because of the torrential rains on July 7 that turned the roads to quagmires of mud. Long detours were required for the III and V Corps, although the disadvantage of the additional distance was offset by the roads' proximity to Frederick, which was connected by the Baltimore and Ohio Railroad to Union supply centers, and by the superior condition of those roads, including the macadamized National Road.[28]

Augustus Van Dyke, 14th Indiana, letter to his father[29]

The Confederate Army's rear guard arrived in Hagerstown on the morning of July 7, screened skillfully by their cavalry, and began to establish defensive positions. By July 11 they occupied a 6-mile line on high ground with their right resting on the Potomac River near Downsville and the left about 1.5 miles southwest of Hagerstown, covering the only road from there to Williamsport. The Conococheague Creek protected the position from any attack that might be launched from the west. They erected impressive earthworks with a 6-foot-wide (1.8 m) parapet on top and frequent gun emplacements, creating comprehensive crossfire zones. Longstreet's Corps occupied the right end of the line, Hill's the center, and Ewell's the left. These works were completed on the morning of July 12, just as the Union army arrived to confront them.[30]

Meade telegraphed to general-in-chief Henry W. Halleck on July 12 that he intended to attack the next day, "unless something intervenes to prevent it." He once again called a council of war with his subordinates on the night of July 12. Of the seven senior officers, only Brig. Gen. James S. Wadsworth and Maj. Gen. Oliver O. Howard were in favor of attacking the Confederate fortifications. Objections centered on the lack of reconnaissance that had been performed. On July 13, Meade and Humphreys scouted the positions personally and issued orders to the corps commanders for a reconnaissance in force on the morning of July 14. This one-day postponement was another instance of delay for which Meade's political enemies castigated him after the campaign. Halleck told Meade that it was "proverbial that councils of war never fight."[31]

Figure 6: *Escape of the Army of Virginia, commanded by General Lee, over the Potomac River near Williamsport, painting by Edwin Forbes*

Across the Potomac

On the morning of July 13, Lee became frustrated waiting for Meade to attack him and was dismayed to see that the Federal troops were digging entrenchments of their own in front of his works. He said impatiently, "That is too long for me; I can not wait for that. ... They have but little courage!" By this time Confederate engineers had completed a new pontoon bridge over the Potomac, which had also subsided enough to be forded. Lee ordered a retreat to start after dark, with Longstreet's and Hill's corps and the artillery to use the pontoon bridge at Falling Waters and Ewell's corps to ford the river at Williamsport.[32]

Meade's orders had stated that the reconnaissance in force by four of his corps would be started by 7 a.m. on July 14, but by this time signs were clear that the enemy had withdrawn. Advancing skirmishers found that the entrenchments were empty. Meade ordered a general pursuit of the Confederates at 8:30 a.m., but very little contact could be made at this late hour. Cavalry under Buford and Kilpatrick attacked the rearguard of Lee's army, Maj. Gen. Henry Heth's division, which was still on a ridge about a mile and a half from Falling Waters. The initial attack caught the Confederates by surprise after a long night with little sleep, and hand-to-hand fighting ensued. Kilpatrick attacked again and Buford struck them in their right and rear. Heth's and Pender's divisions lost as many as 2,000 men as prisoners. Brig. Gen. J. Johnston Pettigrew, who had survived Pickett's Charge with a minor hand wound, was mortally wounded at Falling Waters.[33]

The minor success against Heth did not make up for the extreme frustration in the Lincoln administration about allowing Lee to escape. The president was quoted by John Hay as saying, "We had them within our grasp. We had only to stretch forth our hands and they were ours. And nothing I could say or do could make the Army move."[34]

Shepherdstown and Manassas Gap

Although many descriptions of the Gettysburg Campaign end with Lee's crossing of the Potomac on July 13–14,[35] the two armies did not take up positions across from each other on the Rappahannock River for almost two weeks and the official reports of the armies include the maneuvering and minor clashes along the way. On July 16 the cavalry brigades of Fitzhugh Lee and Chambliss held the fords on the Potomac at Shepherdstown to prevent crossing by the Federal infantry. The cavalry division under David Gregg approached the fords and the Confederates attacked them, but the Union cavalrymen held their position until dark before withdrawing. Meade called this a "spirited contest."[36]

The Army of the Potomac crossed the Potomac River at Harpers Ferry and Berlin (now named Brunswick) on July 17–18. They advanced along the east side of the Blue Ridge Mountains, trying to interpose themselves between Lee's army and Richmond. On July 23, Meade ordered French's III Corps to cut off the retreating Confederate columns at Front Royal, by forcing passage through Manassas Gap. At dawn, French began his attack with the New York Excelsior Brigade, led by Brig. Gen. Francis B. Spinola, against Brig. Gen. Ambrose R. Wright's brigade of Georgians, under the command of Col. Edward J. Walker of the 3rd Georgia Regiment, defending the pass. The fight was slow at first, with the superior Union force using its numbers to push Walker from his defensive position back through the gap. About 4:30 p.m., a strong Union attack drove Walker's men until they were reinforced by Maj. Gen. Robert E. Rodes's division and artillery. By dusk, the poorly coordinated Union attacks were abandoned. During the night, Confederate forces withdrew into the Luray Valley. On July 24, the Union army occupied Front Royal, but Lee's army was safely beyond pursuit.[37]

Aftermath

The retreat from Gettysburg ended the Gettysburg Campaign, Robert E. Lee's final strategic offensive in the Civil War. Afterwards, all combat operations of the Army of Northern Virginia were in reaction to Union initiatives. The Confederates suffered over 5,000 casualties during the retreat, including more than 1,000 captured at Monterey Pass, 1,000 stragglers captured from the wagon train by Gregg's division, 500 at Cunningham's Crossroads, 1,000 captured at Falling Waters, and 460 cavalrymen and 300 infantry and artillery killed, wounded, and missing during the ten days of skirmishes and battles.[38] There were over 1,000 Union casualties—primarily cavalrymen—including losses of 263 from Kilpatrick's division at Hagerstown and 120 from Buford's division at Williamsport.[39] For the entire campaign, Confederate casualties were approximately 27,000, Union 30,100.[40]

Meade was hampered during the retreat and pursuit not only by his alleged timidity and his willingness to defer to the cautious judgment of his subordinate commanders, but because his army was exhausted. The advance to Gettysburg was swift and tiring, followed by the largest battle of the war. The pursuit of Lee was physically demanding, through inclement weather and over difficult roads much longer than his opponent's. Enlistments expired, causing depletion of his ranks, as did the New York Draft Riots, which occupied thousands of men that could have reinforced the Army of the Potomac.[41]

Meade was severely criticized for allowing Lee to escape, just as Maj. Gen. George B. McClellan had done after the Battle of Antietam. Under pressure from Lincoln, he launched two campaigns in the fall of 1863—Bristoe and Mine Run—that attempted to defeat Lee. Both were failures. He also suffered humiliation at the hands of his political enemies in front of the Joint Congressional Committee on the Conduct of the War, questioning his actions at Gettysburg and his failure to defeat Lee during the retreat to the Potomac.[42]

References

- Brown, Kent Masterson. *Retreat from Gettysburg: Lee, Logistics, & the Pennsylvania Campaign*. Chapel Hill: University of North Carolina Press, 2005. ISBN 0-8078-2921-8.
- Coddington, Edwin B. *The Gettysburg Campaign; a study in command*. New York: Scribner's, 1968. ISBN 0-684-84569-5.
- Eicher, David J. *The Longest Night: A Military History of the Civil War*. New York: Simon & Schuster, 2001. ISBN 0-684-84944-5.
- Esposito, Vincent J. *West Point Atlas of American Wars*. New York: Frederick A. Praeger, 1959. OCLC 5890637[43]. The collection of maps (without explanatory text) is available online at the West Point website[44].
- Gottfried, Bradley M. *The Maps of Gettysburg: An Atlas of the Gettysburg Campaign, June 3 – June 13, 1863*. New York: Savas Beatie, 2007. ISBN 978-1-932714-30-2.
- Huntington, Tom. *Pennsylvania Civil War Trails: The Guide to Battle Sites, Monuments, Museums and Towns*. Mechanicsburg, PA: Stackpole Books, 2007. ISBN 978-0-8117-3379-3.
- Kennedy, Frances H., ed. *The Civil War Battlefield Guide*[45]. 2nd ed. Boston: Houghton Mifflin Co., 1998. ISBN 0-395-74012-6.

- Longacre, Edward G. *The Cavalry at Gettysburg*. Lincoln: University of Nebraska Press, 1986. ISBN 0-8032-7941-8.
- Salmon, John S. *The Official Virginia Civil War Battlefield Guide*. Mechanicsburg, PA: Stackpole Books, 2001. ISBN 0-8117-2868-4.
- Sears, Stephen W. *Gettysburg*. Boston: Houghton Mifflin, 2003. ISBN 0-395-86761-4.
- Symonds, Craig L. *American Heritage History of the Battle of Gettysburg*. New York: HarperCollins, 2001. ISBN 0-06-019474-X.
- Wittenberg, Eric J., J. David Petruzzi, and Michael F. Nugent. *One Continuous Fight: The Retreat from Gettysburg and the Pursuit of Lee's Army of Northern Virginia, July 4–14, 1863*. New York: Savas Beatie, 2008. ISBN 978-1-932714-43-2.
- Woodworth, Steven E. *Beneath a Northern Sky: A Short History of the Gettysburg Campaign*. Wilmington, DE: SR Books (scholarly Resources, Inc.), 2003. ISBN 0-8420-2933-8.
- National Park Service battle descriptions[46]

Further reading

- Foote, Shelby. *The Civil War: A Narrative*. Vol. 2, *Fredericksburg to Meridian*. New York: Random House, 1958. ISBN 0-394-49517-9.
- Laino, Philip, *Gettysburg Campaign Atlas*. 2nd ed. Dayton, OH: Gatehouse Press 2009. ISBN 978 1 934900-45-1.
- Petruzzi, J. David, and Steven Stanley. *The Complete Gettysburg Guide*. New York: Savas Beatie, 2009. ISBN 978-1-932714-63-0.

External links

- Animated History of the Gettysburg Campaign[47]

Battle of Fairfield

Battle of Fairfield near Fairfield Gap	
Part of the American Civil War	
Date	July 3, 1863
Location	North of Fairfield, Adams County, Pennsylvania
Result	Confederate victory
Belligerents	
▓▓ USA (Union)	▪ CSA (Confederacy)
Commanders and leaders	
Samuel H. Starr	William E. "Grumble" Jones
Strength	
400	1050 (estimated)
Casualties and losses	
242 (6 killed, 28 wounded, 208 missing)	34 (8 killed, 21 wounded, and 5 missing)

The **Battle of Fairfield** was a cavalry engagement during the Gettysburg Campaign of the American Civil War. It was fought July 3, 1863, near Fairfield, Pennsylvania, concurrently with the Battle of Gettysburg, although it was not a formal part of that battle. While a minor fight by the small number of troops deployed, strategically, the Confederate victory secured the important Hagerstown Road, which Robert E. Lee's Army of Northern Virginia would use on July 5 to return to Maryland and then on to safety in Virginia.

Background

Fairfield had been the site of combat on June 21, when the 14th Virginia Cavalry of Brig. Gen. Albert Jenkins's mounted infantry brigade had used Monterey Pass to conduct a raid near Fairfield with the First Troop, Philadelphia City Cavalry that resulted in the Confederates withdrawing into the Cumberland Valley.

Much of the cavalry of the Army of Northern Virginia had accompanied Maj. Gen. J.E.B. Stuart on his ride around the Union Army of the Potomac through Maryland and south-central Pennsylvania. Lee had retained several brigades to guard the mountain passes as he advanced through the Shenandoah and Cumberland Valleys and to scout Federal positions. Among the latter brigades was that of Brig. Gen. William E. "Grumble" Jones—the celebrated "Laurel Brigade" that had once been commanded by Turner Ashby. Jones had detached one of his best commands, the 35th Battalion, Virginia Cavalry, to accompany the infantry of Jubal Early, but retained the bulk of his command. Jones's Brigade had been raiding the Baltimore & Ohio Railroad in West Virginia and Maryland before being recalled by Lee. They hastened to Pennsylvania, crossing the Potomac River on July 1 (where Jones detached the 12th Virginia Cavalry to guard the ford) and camping at Chambersburg the following night. Jones's force had been reduced to the 6th, 7th, and 11th Virginia Cavalry and Preston Chew's Battery of horse artillery. Jones reached Fairfield on July 3 in response to Lee's orders to secure the vital Hagerstown Road.

Reports of a slow moving Confederate wagon train in the vicinity had attracted the attention of newly commissioned Union Brig. Gen. Wesley Merritt, who ordered the 6th U.S. Cavalry under Maj. Samuel H. Starr to scout Fairfield and locate the wagons. Once in Fairfield, Major Starr learned that a wagon train had just rolled out of town and was heading to Cashtown. He divided his 400 men into three detachments and began to search for the wagons.

Battle

One party soon encountered the pickets of Jones's 7th Virginia Cavalry and withdrew when additional Confederates rode up. Informed of the presence of the enemy, Starr rode to a small ridge and dismounted his men in fields and an orchard on both sides of the road. He threw back a mounted charge of the 7th Virginia, just as Chew's Battery unlimbered and opened fire on the Federal cavalrymen. Supported by the 6th Virginia, the 7th Virginia charged again,[48] clearing Starr's force off the ridge and inflicting heavy losses. Jones pursued the retreating Federals for three miles to the Fairfield Gap, but was unable to catch his quarry.

Aftermath

Federal losses were 6 killed, 28 wounded, and 208 unaccounted for—primarily prisoners. The losses for the Confederates were 8 killed, 21 wounded, and 5 missing.

Jones camped near Fairfield and kept the road open for Lee's retreat, then guarded the rear as the Army of Northern Virginia slogged through the Fairfield Gap in a driving rainstorm on July 5.

Pvt. George C. Platt, an Irish immigrant serving in Troop H of the 6th U.S. Cavalry, was awarded the Medal of Honor on July 12, 1895, for his actions at Fairfield. His citation reads, "Seized the regimental flag upon the death of the standard bearer in a hand-to-hand fight and prevented it from falling into the hands of the enemy."

After the fighting had ended, many wounded soldiers were cared for in the town of Fairfield. Major Samuel H. Starr was taken to the widow Sarah Amanda Blythe's house, which is likely where his arm was amputated. Other accounts mention that the Rufus C. Swope House (across from the Fairfield Inn), and St. John's Lutheran Church were used as hospitals. It is probable that other buildings in the town were used for this purpose as well.

References

- Longacre, Edward G., *The Cavalry at Gettysburg*, University of Nebraska Press, 1986, ISBN 0-8032-7941-8.
- Wittenberg, Eric J., *Gettysburg's Forgotten Cavalry Actions,* Thomas Publications, 1998, ISBN 1-57747-035-4.
- Platt MOH webpage[49]

Fight at Monterey Pass

Fight at Monterey Pass (Gap)	
Part of the American Civil War	
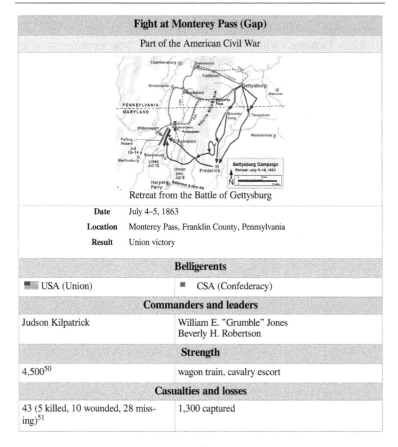 Retreat from the Battle of Gettysburg	
Date	July 4–5, 1863
Location	Monterey Pass, Franklin County, Pennsylvania
Result	Union victory
Belligerents	
USA (Union)	CSA (Confederacy)
Commanders and leaders	
Judson Kilpatrick	William E. "Grumble" Jones Beverly H. Robertson
Strength	
4,500[50]	wagon train, cavalry escort
Casualties and losses	
43 (5 killed, 10 wounded, 28 missing)[51]	1,300 captured

The **Fight at Monterey Pass (or Gap)**[52] was an American Civil War military engagement beginning the evening of July 4, 1863, during the Retreat from Gettysburg. A Confederate wagon train of Lt. Gen. Richard S. Ewell's Second Corps, Army of Northern Virginia, withdrew after the Battle of Gettysburg, and Union cavalry under Brig. Gen. H. Judson Kilpatrick attacked the retreating Confederate column. After a lengthy delay in which a small detachment of Maryland cavalrymen delayed Kilpatrick's division, the Union cavalrymen captured numerous Confederate prisoners and destroyed hundreds of wagons.

Background

General Robert E. Lee ordered his Confederate Army of Northern Virginia to begin withdrawing from Gettysburg following his army's defeat on July 3, 1863. When Maj. Gen. George G. Meade's Army of the Potomac did not counterattack by the evening of July 4, Lee realized that he could accomplish nothing more in his Gettysburg Campaign and that he had to return his battered army to Virginia. His ability to supply his army by living off the Pennsylvania countryside was now significantly reduced and the Union could easily bring up additional reinforcements as time passed, whereas he could not. Prior to the movement of the infantry and artillery, however, Lee was concerned with removing his long train of wagons, supplies, and wounded men over South Mountain and into the Cumberland Valley. He sent the majority of the wagons and ambulances under the direction of Brig. Gen. John D. Imboden over the Chambersburg Pike, which passed through Cashtown in the direction of Chambersburg and Hagerstown, Maryland.[53]

While Imboden's wagons moved northwest, Lee designated a shorter route for his three corps: southwest through Fairfield and over Monterey Pass to Hagerstown. After dark on July 4, Lt. Gen. A.P. Hill's Third Corps headed out onto the Fairfield Road, followed by Lt. Gen. James Longstreet's First Corps and Lt. Gen. Richard S. Ewell's Second Corps. Lee accompanied Hill at the head of the column. Departing in the dark, Lee had the advantage of getting several hours head start and the route from the west side of the battlefield to Williamsport was about half as long as the ones available to the Army of the Potomac.[54]

However, the first traffic on the Fairfield Road had begun on the evening of July 3, when Ewell, concerned about the logistical challenges of the impending retreat, sent his corps trains and herds of captured cattle ahead of his main body. He divided his wagons into three columns. The first used the Cashtown Gap, the second the Fairfield Gap, and the third the Monterey Pass. The wagons headed for Monterey Pass followed the route of Maj. Gen. George Pickett's division, which was moving to the rear as escorts for the Union prisoners of war from the battle.[55]

Early on July 4 Meade sent his cavalry to strike the enemy's rear and lines of communication so as to "harass and annoy him as much as possible in his retreat." Eight cavalry brigades took to the field. Col. J. Irvin Gregg's brigade moved toward Cashtown via Hunterstown and the Mummasburg Road, but all of the others moved south of Gettysburg. Brig. Gen. Judson Kilpatrick's cavalry division joined up with the brigade of Col. Pennock Huey at Emmitsburg, Maryland, and they were ordered to locate and destroy "a heavy train of wagons" that had been spotted by a Union signal station. Assuming that

Figure 7: *Brig. Gen. Judson Kilpatrick*

Ewell's corps wagon train was actually the main supply trains for Lee's army,
Kilpatrick moved out aggressively at 10 a.m. on July 4, proceeding west on
the Waynesboro-Emmitsburg Turnpike toward the village of Fountain Dale
(just east of present-day Blue Ridge Summit on Pennsylvania Route 16) and
Monterey Pass.[56]

Confederate cavalry commander Maj. Gen. J.E.B. Stuart understood the im-
portance of securing the mountain passes and he assigned the primary responsibility to the cavalry brigades of Brig. Gens. Beverly H. Robertson and
William E. "Grumble" Jones. Recognizing the vulnerability of Ewell's im-
mense wagon train in the narrow Monterey Pass, Jones asked permission from
Stuart to use his entire brigade to defend it. Stuart allowed the 6th and 7th
Virginia Cavalry regiments and a battery of horse artillery under Capt. Roger
Preston Chew to be assigned. The 7th Virginia was soon recalled, replaced by
the 4th North Carolina Cavalry of Robertson's Brigade.[57]

Engagement in the Pass

Brig. Gen. George A. Custer, a brigade commander under Kilpatrick, received intelligence from a local civilian that the rear of Ewell's wagon train
was approaching a large summer resort hotel named Monterey Springs, which
sat atop the Pass. Despite being warned of a Confederate artillery placement

Figure 8: *Brig. Gen. William E. "Grumble" Jones*

ahead, Kilpatrick ordered his entire force to advance. A single 12-pounder Napoleon of Courtney's Battery fired a shot at the Union horsemen, but the gunners withdrew before they could be attacked.[58]

The remaining Confederate force on the road up the hill to the Pass consisted of a detachment of 20 dismounted cavalrymen under Capt. George M. Emack from the 1st Maryland Cavalry Battalion, along with a single cannon. As Union troopers from the 5th Michigan Cavalry approached Emack's men, the cannon opened fire and eight of the Marylanders conducted a mounted charge into the head of the Union column. In the dark and the heavy rain, the Union cavalrymen were taken by surprise and many of them retreated in panic. The Confederate cavalrymen dismounted and took up positions on both sides of the road. When the Federals returned, Emack's men waited patiently until they were about 10 yards away and opened fire. The Union cavalrymen were convinced they were opposed by a much larger force. While this standoff continued, Ewell's wagons were moving as swiftly as possible to get out of range of the Union cavalry threat.[59]

By the time Grumble Jones was able to make his way to the scene through the crowded roads, the small Maryland detachment had been driven back several hundred yards, almost to the road junction being used by the wagon train. By this time less than one half of the train had made it safely through the Pass.

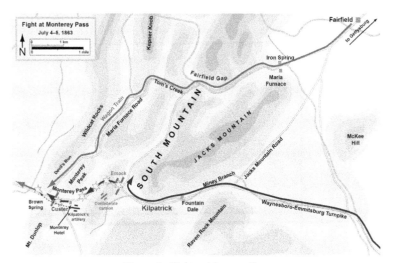

Figure 9: *Fight at Monterey Pass*

Jones promised reinforcements from the 6th Virginia Cavalry and Emack ordered his men to hold their ground and conserve their ammunition. Meanwhile, elements of Jones's cavalry attacked Huey's brigade in the rear of Kilpatrick's column.[60]

Kilpatrick brought forward two guns of horse artillery from Lt. Alexander C. M. Pennington's Battery M, 2nd U.S. Artillery, supported by men of the 1st Ohio Cavalry. South of the hotel, a bridge on the road had not been destroyed by the Confederates and Col. Russell A. Alger of the 5th Michigan Cavalry requested reinforcements to make a mounted charge across the bridge. Kilpatrick ordered Custer to make the attack with his full Michigan Brigade. The advance of the 5th and 6th Michigan Cavalry regiments was slowed by the darkness, difficult terrain, and dense undergrowth. The tiny group of Marylanders, supported by a few cavalrymen from the 4th North Carolina of Robertson's Brigade, had delayed the Union advance for nearly five hours.[61]

At about 3 a.m. on July 5, as the Michigan Brigade continued to move slowly forward, Kilpatrick sent in the 1st West Virginia Cavalry under Major Charles E. Capehart. Capehart's 640 officers and men charged what they imagined to be "five times" their numbers. In hand-to-hand fighting with sabers and revolvers, they seized the Confederate cannon and Capehart was later awarded the Medal of Honor for his gallant service. The road was open to attack the wagon train.[62]

Attacking the wagon train

The Union cavalrymen crashed into the column of now lightly protected wagons. Custer, in his enthusiasm for the charge, was thrown from his horse and nearly captured. Grumble Jones also narrowly avoided capture. Pennington's artillery began shelling the wagons toward the rear of the column, splintering carriages and blocking any opportunity for retreat. The Union and Confederate cavalrymen became thoroughly mixed up among the wagons and the enemies were unable to differentiate themselves in the darkness. Several friendly fire incidents occurred as Union troopers accidentally fired on their own lines.[63]

Union troopers rode all the way through the wagon train until they reached Ewell's infantry and captured large numbers of prisoners before returning to repeat the effort. They erected hasty barricades in front of the wagon train to protect what they had captured. More than 1,300 Confederates—primarily wounded men in ambulances, but also slaves, free blacks, and some cavalrymen—were captured and most of the wagons were destroyed. Many of the mules survived and were turned over to the Cavalry Corps quartermaster. Kilpatrick later reported that he had destroyed Ewell's entire wagon train, although he had in fact encountered only a fraction of the full, 40-mile long train. The Confederates lost about 250 wagons and ambulances with casualties from Iverson's and Daniel's Brigades and of three artillery battalions, as well as 37 wagons from Maj. Gen. Robert E. Rodes's division quartermaster trains.[64]

Aftermath

Following the fight at Monterrey, Kirkpatrick's division reached Smithsburg around 2 p.m. on July 5. Stuart arrived from over South Mountain with the brigades of Chambliss and Ferguson. A horse artillery duel ensued, causing some damage to the small town. Kilpatrick withdrew at dark "to save my prisoners, animals, and wagons" and arrived at Boonsboro (spelled Boonsborough at that time) before midnight.[65]

Lee's retreat continued to the Potomac, as minor combat operations—primarily cavalry actions—occurred at Hagerstown (July 6 and 12), Boonsboro (July 8), Funkstown (July 7 and 10), and around Williamsport and Falling Waters (July 6–14). At the Potomac, the Confederates found that rising waters and destroyed pontoon bridges prevented their immediate crossing. Erecting substantial defensive works, they awaited to the arrival of the Union army, which had been pursuing over longer roads more to the south of Lee's route. Before Meade could perform adequate reconnaissance and attack the Confederate fortifications, Lee's army escaped across fords and a hastily rebuilt bridge.[66]

In popular media

A 40-minute documentary on the battle entitled *Ten Days and Still They Come
— The Battle at Monterey Pass* was released in 2011.[67]

References

- Brown, Kent Masterson. *Retreat from Gettysburg: Lee, Logistics, & the
  Pennsylvania Campaign*. Chapel Hill: University of North Carolina Press,
  2005. ISBN 0-8078-2921-8.
- Coddington, Edwin B. *The Gettysburg Campaign; a study in command*.
  New York: Scribner's, 1968. ISBN 0-684-84569-5.
- Gottfried, Bradley M. *The Maps of Gettysburg: An Atlas of the Gettys-
  burg Campaign, June 3 – June 13, 1863*. New York: Savas Beatie, 2007.
  ISBN 978-1-932714-30-2.
- Huntington, Tom. *Pennsylvania Civil War Trails: The Guide to Battle
  Sites, Monuments, Museums and Towns*. Mechanicsburg, PA: Stackpole
  Books, 2007. ISBN 978-0-8117-3379-3.
- Longacre, Edward G. *The Cavalry at Gettysburg*. Lincoln: University of
  Nebraska Press, 1986. ISBN 0-8032-7941-8.
- Wittenberg, Eric J., J. David Petruzzi, and Michael F. Nugent. *One Con-
  tinuous Fight: The Retreat from Gettysburg and the Pursuit of Lee's
  Army of Northern Virginia, July 4–14, 1863*. New York: Savas Beatie,
  2008. ISBN 978-1-932714-43-2.

Further reading

 Wikimedia Commons has media related to *Pennsylvania in the American Civil War*.

- Laino, Philip, *Gettysburg Campaign Atlas*. 2nd ed. Dayton, OH: Gate-
  house Press 2009. ISBN 978-1-934900-45-1.
- Wert, Jeffry D. *Custer: The Controversial Life of George Armstrong
  Custer*. New York: Simon & Schuster, 1997. ISBN 978-0-684-83275-3.

External links

- Miller, John Allen, *Monterey Pass: The Gateway of Agony*[68], Emmitsburg
  Area Historical Society website, accessed March 9, 2009.
- Monterey Pass Battlefield Association[69]
- Monterey Pass Battlefield Park[70]

Battle of Williamsport

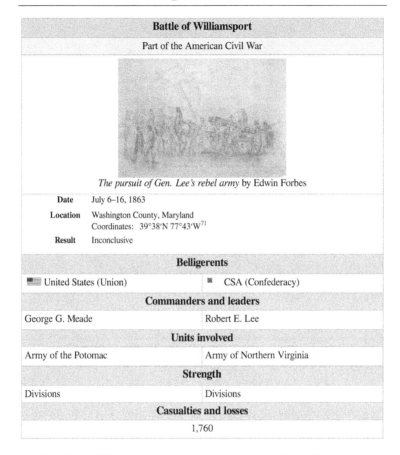

Battle of Williamsport	
Part of the American Civil War	
The pursuit of Gen. Lee's rebel army by Edwin Forbes	
Date	July 6–16, 1863
Location	Washington County, Maryland Coordinates: 39°38′N 77°43′W[71]
Result	Inconclusive
Belligerents	
United States (Union)	CSA (Confederacy)
Commanders and leaders	
George G. Meade	Robert E. Lee
Units involved	
Army of the Potomac	Army of Northern Virginia
Strength	
Divisions	Divisions
Casualties and losses	
1,760	

The **Battle of Williamsport**, also known as the **Battle of Hagerstown** or **Falling Waters**, took place from July 6 to July 16, 1863, in Washington County, Maryland, as part of the Gettysburg Campaign of the American Civil War. It's not to be confused with the fighting at Hoke's Run which was also known as the Battle of Falling Waters

During the night of July 4–July 5, Gen. Robert E. Lee's battered Confederate army began its retreat from Gettysburg, moving southwest on the Fairfield Road toward Hagerstown and Williamsport, screened by Maj. Gen. J.E.B. Stuart's cavalry. The Union infantry followed cautiously the next day, converging on Middletown, Maryland.

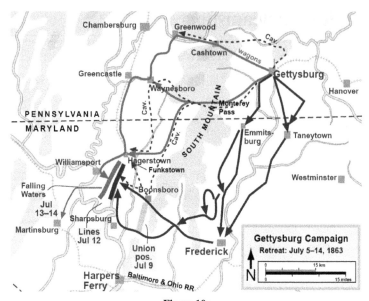

Figure 10:
Gettysburg Campaign (July 5– July 14)
Confederate
Union

By July 7, Brig. Gen. John D. Imboden stopped Brig. Gen. John Buford's Union cavalry from occupying Williamsport and destroying Confederate trains. On July 6, Brig. Gen. Judson Kilpatrick's cavalry division drove two Confederate cavalry brigades through Hagerstown before being forced to retire by the arrival of the rest of Stuart's command. Lee's infantry reached the rain-swollen Potomac River but could not cross, the pontoon bridge having been destroyed by a cavalry raid.

On July 11, Lee entrenched a line, protecting the river crossings at Williamsport and waited for Maj. Gen. George G. Meade's Army of the Potomac to advance. On July 12, Meade reached the vicinity and probed the Confederate line. On July 13, skirmishing was heavy along the lines as Meade positioned his forces for an attack. In the meantime, the river fell enough to allow the construction of a new bridge, and Lee's army began crossing the river after dark on the 13th.

On the morning of July 14, Kilpatrick's and Buford's cavalry divisions approached from the north and east respectively. Before allowing Buford to gain a position on the flank and rear, Kilpatrick attacked the rearguard division of

Maj. Gen. Henry Heth taking more than 500 prisoners. Confederate Brig. Gen. J. Johnston Pettigrew was mortally wounded in the fight.

On July 16, Brig. Gen. David McM. Gregg's cavalry approached Shepherdstown where the brigades of Brig. Gens. Fitzhugh Lee and John R. Chambliss, supported by Col. Milton J. Ferguson's brigade, held the Potomac River fords against the Union infantry. Fitzhugh Lee and Chambliss attacked Gregg, who held out against several attacks and sorties, fighting sporadically until nightfall when he withdrew.

References

- National Park Service battle description[72]

Battle of Boonsboro

Battle of Boonsboro	
Part of the American Civil War	
Date	July 8, 1863
Location	Washington County, Maryland Coordinates: 39.5254°N 77.6632°W[73]
Result	Inconclusive
Belligerents	
▓▓ United States (Union)	▪ CSA (Confederacy)
Commanders and leaders	
Alfred Pleasonton	J.E.B. Stuart
Strength	
Divisions	Divisions
Casualties and losses	
100	

The **Battle of Boonsboro** took place on July 8, 1863, in Washington County, Maryland, as part of the Retreat from Gettysburg during the Gettysburg Campaign of the American Civil War.

While Gen. Robert E. Lee's Army of Northern Virginia retreated toward Virginia following its defeat in the Battle of Gettysburg, Confederate cavalry held the South Mountain passes. The cavalry fought a rearguard action against elements of the Union 1st and 3rd Cavalry Divisions and supporting infantry. This action was one of a series of successive cavalry engagements around Boonsboro, Hagerstown, and Williamsport.

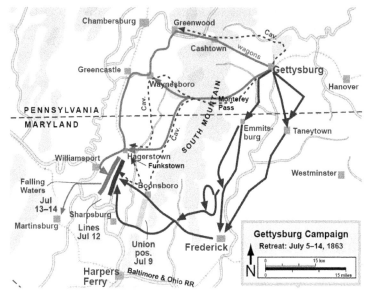

Figure 11:
Gettysburg Campaign (July 5–14)
Confederate
Union

Battle

Confederate Maj. Gen. J.E.B. Stuart faced a difficult assignment—locate the Union cavalry and prevent it from severing Gen. Lee's avenue of retreat to Williamsport and the Potomac River. The result was the biggest and most sustained cavalry battle in Maryland during the campaign. The Battle of Boonsboro occurred along the National Road on Wednesday, July 8, 1863.

Stuart, with five cavalry brigades, advanced from the direction of Funkstown and Williamsport. He first encountered Federal resistance at Beaver Creek Bridge, 4.5 miles (7.2 km) north of Boonsboro. By 11 a.m., the Confederate cavalry had pushed forward to several mud-soaked fields, where fighting on horseback was nearly impossible, forcing Stuart's troopers and Brig. Gens. H. Judson Kilpatrick's and John Buford's Union cavalry divisions to dismount and slug it out like infantry.

By mid-afternoon, the Union left under Kilpatrick crumbled as the Federals ran low on ammunition under increasing Confederate pressure. Stuart's advanced ended about 7 p.m., however, when Union infantry arrived—the first to engage in battle since Gettysburg. Stuart withdrew north to Funkstown, but he had gained another day for Lee's retreating army. Two days later, he would again delay the Federal pursuit at the Battle of Funkstown.[74]

References

* National Park Service battle description[75]

Battle of Funkstown

Second Battle of Funkstown	
Part of the American Civil War	
Date	July 10, 1863
Location	Funkstown, Maryland
Result	Confederate victory
Belligerents	
United States (Union)	CSA (Confederacy)
Commanders and leaders	
John Buford	J.E.B. Stuart
Strength	
1 cavalry division 1 infantry brigade	1 cavalry division 1 infantry brigade
Casualties and losses	
479	

The **Second Battle of Funkstown** (more commonly simply referred to as the **Battle of Funkstown**) took place near Funkstown, Maryland, on July 10, 1863, during the Gettysburg Campaign of the American Civil War. Union forces of the Army of the Potomac attacked the rear guard of the Confederate Army of Northern Virginia during its retreat from Pennsylvania following the Battle of Gettysburg.

A strong Confederate presence at Funkstown threatened any Union advance against Gen. Robert E. Lee's position near Williamsport and the Potomac River as he retreated to Virginia after the Battle of Gettysburg. Maj. Gen. J.E.B. Stuart's cavalry, posted at Funkstown, posed a serious risk to the Federal right and rear if the Union army lunged west from Boonsboro. Stuart, meanwhile, determined to wage a spirited defense to ensure Lee time to complete fortifications protecting his army and his avenue of retreat.[76]

As Brig. Gen. John Buford's Federal cavalry division cautiously approached Funkstown via the National Road on Friday morning July 10, 1863, it encountered Stuart's crescent-shaped, three-mile-long battle line. It was Stuart's first

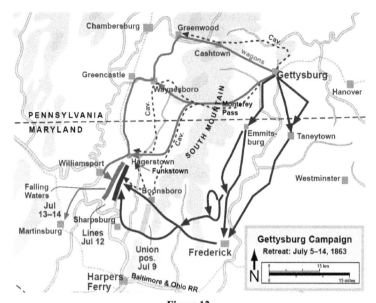

Figure 12:
Gettysburg Campaign (July 5– July 14)
Confederate
Union

defensive battle since reentering Maryland. The high ground constituted Stuart's extreme right, held by Preston Chew's horse artillery. A nearby stone barn and barnyard wall proved a superb defensive position for the 34th Virginia Battalion's dismounted cavalry.

Col. Thomas C. Devin's dismounted Union cavalry brigade attacked about 8:00 a.m. By mid-afternoon, with Buford's cavalrymen running low on ammunition and gaining little ground, Col. Lewis A. Grant's First Vermont Brigade of infantry arrived and jabbed at the Confederate center less than one mile away. Unbeknownst to the Vermonters, Gen. George T. Anderson's Confederate brigade now faced them, the first time opposing infantry had clashed since the Battle of Gettysburg.

By early evening, the Union Army began withdrawing south towards Beaver Creek, where the Union I, VI, and XI Corps had concentrated. Stuart had kept the Federals at bay for yet another day.

The day-long battle east of the road resulted in 479 casualties. The Chaney house served as a hospital. At the Keller home, Confederate Major Henry D. McDaniel, later the governor of Georgia, survived his wounds. He would spend the rest of the war in a Union prisoner-of-war camp.[77]

A smaller engagement took place near Funkstown on July 7, three days prior to the Battle of Funkstown.

References

- Maryland Civil War Trails wayside marker for the Battle of Funkstown[78]

Notes

Coordinates: 39.60592°N 77.700462°W[79]

Meade Pursues

Battle of Manassas Gap

Battle of Manassas Gap	
Part of the American Civil War	
Date	July 23, 1863
Location	Warren County, Virginia
Result	Inconclusive
Belligerents	
▄▄ United States (Union)	▄ CSA (Confederacy)
Commanders and leaders	
William H. French	Richard H. Anderson
Strength	
Divisions	Divisions
Casualties and losses	
440[80]	

The **Battle of Manassas Gap**, also known as the **Battle of Wapping Heights**, took place on July 23, 1863, in Warren County, Virginia, at the conclusion of General Robert E. Lee's retreat back to Virginia in the final days of the Gettysburg Campaign of the American Civil War. Union forces attempted to force passage across the Blue Ridge Mountains and attack the Confederate rear as it formed a defensive position in the upper Shenandoah Valley. Despite successfully forcing the passage at Manassas Gap, the Union force was unable to do so before Lee retreated further up the valley to safety, resulting in an inconclusive battle.

Background

Following their defeat at the Battle of Gettysburg, Lee's Confederate Army of Northern Virginia retreated across the Potomac River at Williamsport, Maryland, and withdrew into the Shenandoah Valley. Maj. Gen. George G. Meade's Army of the Potomac, in pursuit of Lee's broken army, decided to try to flank the Confederate army by crossing the river east of the Blue Ridge Mountains at Harpers Ferry and Berlin, Maryland, into the Loudoun Valley and then forcing a passage across the Blue Ridge in Lee's rear. To this end, on July 23, Meade ordered the III Corps, under Maj. Gen. William H. French, to cut off the retreating Confederate columns at Front Royal, Virginia, by forcing passage through Manassas Gap.

Battle

At dawn, French began his attack with the New York Excelsior Brigade, led by Brig. Gen. Francis B. Spinola, against Brig. Gen. Ambrose R. Wright's brigade of Georgians, under the command of Col. Edward J. Walker of the 3rd Georgia Regiment, defending the pass. The fight was slow at first, with the superior Union force using its numbers to push Walker from his defensive position back through the gap. In the late afternoon, around 4:30 p.m., French made a concerted assault on Walker's brigade, driving them from the gap. The Confederates were quickly reinforced by Maj. Gen. Robert E. Rodes's division and artillery, stalling the Union advance. By dusk, the Union attack became uncoordinated and was abandoned. During the night, Confederate forces withdrew into the Luray Valley. On July 24, the Union army occupied Front Royal, but Lee's army was safely beyond pursuit.[81]

Aftermath

The small fight was inconclusive. The Union army was able to successfully gain passage through the gap in the Blue Ridge and occupy Front Royal, but not before Lee was able to withdraw further up the valley to safety. By failing to cut off the Confederate retreat and bring Lee into battle, the Army of Northern Virginia was allowed to reorganize and regroup. By the end of the summer both armies had taken their familiar positions opposite the Rappahannock and Rapidan rivers, setting the stage for the Bristoe and Mine Run campaigns in the fall.

References

- Kennedy, Frances H., ed. *The Civil War Battlefield Guide*. 2nd ed. Boston: Houghton Mifflin Co., 1998. ISBN 0-395-74012-6.
- Salmon, John S. *The Official Virginia Civil War Battlefield Guide*. Mechanicsburg, PA: Stackpole Books, 2001. ISBN 0-8117-2868-4.
- National Park Service battle description[82]

Coordinates: 38.914°N 78.114°W[83]

Bristoe Campaign

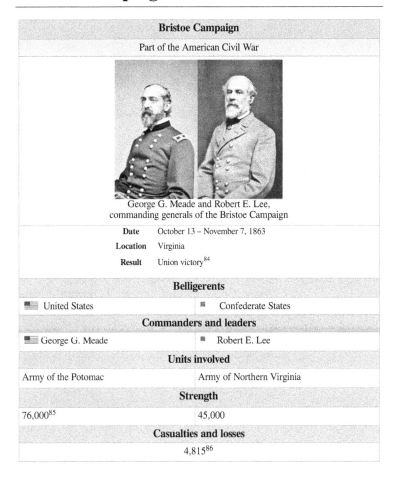

Bristoe Campaign	
Part of the American Civil War	
George G. Meade and Robert E. Lee, commanding generals of the Bristoe Campaign	
Date	October 13 – November 7, 1863
Location	Virginia
Result	Union victory[84]
Belligerents	
United States	Confederate States
Commanders and leaders	
George G. Meade	Robert E. Lee
Units involved	
Army of the Potomac	Army of Northern Virginia
Strength	
76,000[85]	45,000
Casualties and losses	
4,815[86]	

The **Bristoe Campaign** was a series of minor battles fought in Virginia during October and November 1863, in the American Civil War. Maj. Gen. George G. Meade, commanding the Union Army of the Potomac, began to maneuver in an unsuccessful attempt to defeat Gen. Robert E. Lee's Army of Northern Virginia. Lee countered with a turning movement, which caused Meade to withdraw his army back toward Centreville. Lee struck at Bristoe Station on October 14, but suffered losses in two brigades and withdrew. As Meade followed south once again, the Union army smashed a Confederate defensive bridgehead at Rappahannock Station on November 7 and drove Lee back across the Rapidan River. Along with the infantry battles, the cavalry forces of the armies fought at Auburn on October 13, again at Auburn on October 14, and at Buckland Mills on October 19.

The Confederates had not achieved their primary objectives of bringing on a decisive battle or preventing the Federal reinforcement of the Western Theater, and Lee and his officers were much demoralized by this failure.

Background

After the Battle of Gettysburg in July, Robert E. Lee retreated back across the Potomac River to Virginia and concentrated behind the Rapidan River in Orange County, Virginia. Meade was widely criticized for failing to pursue aggressively and defeat Lee's army. He planned new offensives in Virginia for the fall.

Early in September, Lee dispatched two divisions of Lt. Gen. James Longstreet's Corps to reinforce the Confederate Army of Tennessee for the Battle of Chickamauga. Meade knew that Lee had been weakened by the departure of Longstreet and wanted to take advantage. Meade advanced his army to the Rappahannock River in August, and on September 13 he pushed strong columns forward to confront Lee along the Rapidan, occupying Culpeper, Virginia, following the Battle of Culpeper Court House. Meade planned to use his numerical superiority in a broad turning movement, similar to the one planned by Maj. Gen. Joseph Hooker in the Battle of Chancellorsville that spring. However, on September 24 the Union had to deplete its forces as well, sending the XI and XII Corps to the Chattanooga Campaign in Tennessee.

Lee learned of the departing Union corps, and early in October he began an offensive sweep around Cedar Mountain with his remaining two corps, attempting to turn Meade's right flank. Meade, despite having superior numbers, did not wish to give battle in a position that did not offer him the advantage and ordered the Army of the Potomac to withdraw along the line of the Orange and Alexandria Railroad.

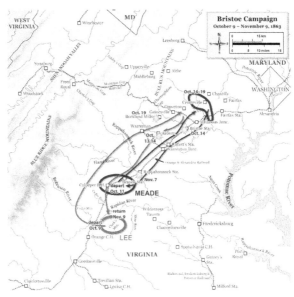

Figure 13:
Bristoe Campaign
Confederate
Union

Opposing forces

Battles

Auburn (October 13–14)

On October 13, Maj. Gen. J.E.B. Stuart was on one of his typical cavalry raids to capture supply wagons and blundered into the rear guard of the Union III Corps near Warrenton. Lt. Gen. Richard S. Ewell's corps was sent to rescue him, but Stuart hid his troopers in a wooded ravine until the unsuspecting III Corps moved on, and the assistance was not necessary.[87]

As the Union army withdrew towards Manassas Junction, Meade was careful to protect his western flank from the kind of envelopment that had doomed Maj. Gen. John Pope and Hooker in previous battles in this area. Brigades from Maj. Gen. Gouverneur K. Warren's II Corps fought a rearguard action against Stuart's cavalry and the infantry of Brig. Gen. Harry Hays's division near Auburn on October 14. Stuart's cavalry boldly bluffed Warren's infantry and escaped disaster. The II Corps pushed on to Catlett Station on the Orange & Alexandria Railroad.[88]

Bristoe Station (October 14)

Lt. Gen. A.P. Hill's corps stumbled upon two corps of the retreating Union army at Bristoe Station and attacked without proper reconnaissance. On October 14, Union soldiers of the II Corps, posted behind the Orange & Alexandria Railroad embankment, mauled two brigades of Maj. Gen. Henry Heth's division and captured a battery of artillery. Hill reinforced his line but could make little headway against the determined defenders. After this victory, Meade continued his withdrawal to Centreville unmolested. Lee's Bristoe offensive sputtered to a premature halt. Meade was well entrenched, and Lee had outrun his supplies. After minor skirmishing near Manassas and Centreville, the Confederates retired slowly to the Rappahannock River, destroying the Orange & Alexandria Railroad as they went. Meade was under pressure from general-in-chief Maj. Gen. Henry W. Halleck to pursue Lee, but it took almost a month to re-lay the railroad track behind his army.[89]

Buckland Races (October 19)

After defeat at Bristoe Station and an aborted advance on Centreville, Stuart's cavalry shielded the withdrawal of Lee's army from the vicinity of Manassas Junction. Union cavalry under Brig. Gen. Judson Kilpatrick pursued Stuart's cavalry along the Warrenton Turnpike but were lured into an ambush near Chestnut Hill and routed. The Federal troopers were scattered and chased five miles (8 km) in an affair that came to be known as the "Buckland Races".[90]

Across the Rappahannock (November 7)

Lee returned to his old position behind the Rappahannock but left a fortified bridgehead on the north bank, protecting the approach to Kelly's Ford. On November 7, Meade forced passage of the Rappahannock at two places. A surprise attack by Maj. Gen. John Sedgwick's VI Corps at dusk overran the Confederate bridgehead at Rappahannock Station, capturing two brigades (more than 1,600 men) of Maj. Gen. Jubal A. Early's division. Fighting at Kelly's Ford was less severe, but the Confederates retreated, allowing the Federals across in force.[91]

Aftermath

On the verge of going into winter quarters around Culpeper, Lee's army retired instead into Orange County, south of the Rapidan. The Army of the Potomac occupied the vicinity of Brandy Station and Culpeper County.

The five battles in the Bristoe Campaign resulted in 4,815 casualties on both sides, including 1,973 Confederate prisoners at Rappahannock Station. Lee and his officers were disgusted with their lack of success. They had not achieved their primary objectives of bringing on a decisive battle or preventing the Federal reinforcement of the Western Theater. Meade's army was in a good position, sitting on their supply base and having suffered fewer casualties in their larger force. Pressured by Abraham Lincoln to achieve an offensive success against Lee before the winter brought campaigning to a halt, Meade began to plan his Mine Run Campaign for later in November.[92]

References

- National Park Service battle descriptions[93]
- Kennedy, Frances H., ed. *The Civil War Battlefield Guide*. 2nd ed. Boston: Houghton Mifflin Co., 1998. ISBN 0-395-74012-6.
- Salmon, John S. *The Official Virginia Civil War Battlefield Guide*. Mechanicsburg, PA: Stackpole Books, 2001. ISBN 0-8117-2868-4.

Further reading

- Henderson, William D. *The Road to Bristoe Station: Campaigning with Lee and Meade, August 1–October 20, 1863*. Lynchburg, VA: H. E. Howard, 1987. ISBN 978-0-930919-45-0.
- Tighe, Adrian G. *The Bristoe Campaign: General Lee's Last Strategic Offensive with the Army of Northern Virginia, October 1863*. Bloomington, IN, Xlibris, 2011. ISBN 978-1-4568-8869-5.

External links

- Orrison, Rob (December 3, 2013). ""I would save him the trouble" – Robert E. Lee's Struggle of Supply in the Fall 1863 Campaign"[94]. Emerging Civil War Blog. Retrieved 7 August 2016.

First Battle of Auburn

First Battle of Auburn	
Part of the American Civil War	
Date October 13, 1863	
Location Fauquier County, Virginia	
Result Inconclusive	
Belligerents	
▓ United States (Union)	▪ CSA (Confederacy)
Commanders and leaders	
William H. French	J.E.B. Stuart
Strength	
2,000	3,000
Casualties and losses	
50	

File:USA Virginia location map.svg
Location of the battle in Virginia

The **First Battle of Auburn** was fought on October 13, 1863, between Union infantry and Confederate cavalry forces at the start of the Bristoe Campaign during the American Civil War. A Union infantry column stumbled upon a Confederate cavalry reconnaissance party and a short, inconclusive fight ensued. The Confederate cavalry withdrew in the face of the superior Union force, but a much larger body of Confederate cavalry under Maj. Gen. J.E.B. Stuart, attempting to raid a Union wagon train became entrapped by the column, forcing them to abandon the raid and hide in a ravine overnight awaiting Confederate infantry to come to their aid.

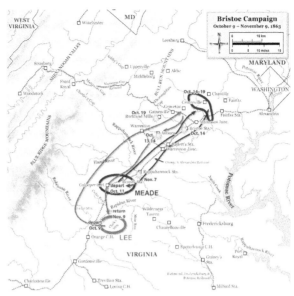

Figure 14:
Bristoe Campaign
Confederate
Union

Background

Following the conclusion of the Gettysburg Campaign, the Confederate Army
of Northern Virginia and Union Army of the Potomac regrouped on their previous positions astride opposite banks of the Rapidan River. For the duration
of the summer both armies remained inactive, reorganizing and resupplying
after the devastation wrought at Gettysburg. In early September, Lt. Gen.
James Longstreet was dispatched with two divisions to aid the Confederate
war effort in the West. After the Confederate victory at Chickamauga, which
Longstreet helped secure, Maj. Gen. George Meade was forced to send the XI
and XII Corps to help secure Middle Tennessee. When Gen. Robert E. Lee
learned of the reassignment of the two Union Corps he decided to go on the
offensive and force the Army of the Potomac to give battle on ground of his
choosing.

Lee's plan was much the same as that of the Northern Virginia Campaign the
year prior: turn the Union right flank by threatening Washington, D.C., using a forced march to the west around the Union line. To that end Lt. Gen.
Richard Ewell's and Lt. Gen. A.P. Hill's corps were ordered to sweep around

the Union right flank, Maj. Gen. Fitzhugh Lee, with three brigades of cavalry and infantry each, was to secure the Rapidan and prevent a Union advance into central Virginia, and Maj. Gen. J.E.B. Stuart was to lead the cavalry in advance of the infantry. The Confederate advance began on October 8 and was almost immediately detected by Union spies and the signaling station atop Cedar Mountain. Unsure of whether Lee was attempting to turn his right flank or make a retrograde movement toward Richmond, Meade ordered dispositions to counter either threat.

The offensive began on October 10 when Stuart led a diversionary attack on Brig. Gen. George A. Custer's division holding the Robinson River west of Culpeper Courthouse. This movement convinced Meade that Lee did not intend to fall back toward Richmond, and Meade moved back on Rappahannock Station to counter Lee's movement. On October 12 Confederate infantry were spotted at Amissville, convincing Meade that Lee planned to send his army through Thoroughfare Gap as he had in 1862. Accordingly, Meade retreated toward Centreville along the Orange and Alexandria Railroad to defend Washington from such a movement. Lee, however, intended to converge on Warrenton and stay to the south of the Bull Run Mountains. On October 13, Stuart was dispatched to reconnoiter the position of the Union left flank as it withdrew toward Centreville.

Battle

At 10 a.m. on October 12, Stuart sent Brig. Gen. Lunsford L. Lomax's brigade east from Warrenton. Stuart followed an hour later with two divisions. Lomax stopped at Auburn to wait for Stuart and dispatched scouts further east who soon discovered Brig. Gen. John Buford's cavalry at Warrenton Junction, guarding the Federal wagon train advancing east by the O&A railroad. No scouts were dispatched to the south however, and the presence of the Union II and III Corps, which had become separated from the main body of the Union army due to confusion during the frequent repositioning of the past few days, marching north toward Auburn.Wikipedia:Please clarify

Stuart arrived at Auburn around 1 p.m. and then rode east to Catlett's Station to reconnoiter the Union wagon train, leaving Lomax to hold Auburn and dispatching his aide, Capt. William B. Blackford to scout to the south of Auburn. Blackford got lost and failed to discover the approaching Federal column. Stuart, meanwhile, impressed by the size of the wagon train, sent a dispatch to Fitzhugh Lee at Warrenton, ordering him to aid in the attack. Lee left Warrenton at 4 p.m. and followed Stuart's path through Auburn.

The Union column led by Maj. Gen. William H. French's III Corps, followed by Brig. Gen. Gouverneur K. Warren's II Corps, approached Auburn about 4:15 p.m. French had dispatched his cavalry under Brig. Gen. H. Judson Kilpatrick to the north to guard his left flank from Confederate cavalry at Warrenton, leaving the column without the cavalry at its head, thus allowing it to stumble into the Confederates at Auburn. French and his staff, at the head of the column, fired their revolvers at the Confederates as the infantry and artillery were brought up. Lomax attempted to charge the Federal line but a volley of canister shot drove back the assault. By 4:45 the fighting died down, just as Lee arrived from Warrenton. Seeing they were facing two infantry corps, Lee and Lomax withdrew to Warrenton.

Aftermath

The short fight resulted in only about 50 casualties, but had deep repercussions for Stuart and the developing campaign. Blackford, finally alerted to the presence of the Federals, notified Stuart of the situation. Seeing that he was trapped between the II and III Corps to his northwest and the wagon train to the southeast, Stuart led his command, some 3,000 men and horses, five ordnance wagons, and seven artillery pieces, into a wooded ravine east of Auburn, only 300 yards (270 m) from Warren's bivouac. After dark, Stuart sent six scouts dressed in Federal uniforms through the Union lines to get word to Robert E. Lee. Lee accordingly dispatched Ewell to Auburn at dawn to rescue Stuart and his cavalry setting up the Second Battle of Auburn the following day.

References

- Salmon, John S., *The Official Virginia Civil War Battlefield Guide*, Stackpole Books, 2001, ISBN 0-8117-2868-4, pp. 217–30

External links

- National Park Service battle description[95]
- CWSAC Report Update[96]

Coordinates: 38.7°N 77.7°W[97]

Second Battle of Auburn

Coordinates: 38.70213°N 77.70181°W[98]

Second Battle of Auburn	
Part of the American Civil War	
Date	October 14, 1863
Location	Fauquier County, Virginia
Result	Inconclusive
Belligerents	
United States of America	Confederate States of America
Commanders and leaders	
Gouverneur K. Warren	J.E.B. Stuart
Strength	
unknown	3,000
Casualties and losses	
113	

File:USA Virginia location map.svg
Location of the battle in Virginia

The **Second Battle of Auburn** was fought on October 14, 1863, in Fauquier County, Virginia, between Union and Confederate forces in the American Civil War. Confederate forces led by Lt. Gen. Richard S. Ewell led a sortie to extricate Maj. Gen. J.E.B. Stuart's cavalry command, trapped between two Union columns and clashed with the rearguard of the Federal II Corps under Brig. Gen. Gouverneur K. Warren. Stuart was successfully extricated but the Federal wagon train avoided Confederate capture in the inconclusive fight.

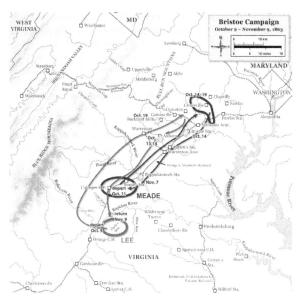

Figure 15:
Bristoe Campaign
Confederate
Union

Background

On October 10, 1863, Gen. Robert E. Lee went on the offensive for the first time since the Gettysburg Campaign in an attempt to turn the right flank of the Army of the Potomac standing between his Army of Northern Virginia and Washington, D.C, much as he had done the year prior during the Northern Virginia Campaign. As Lee began his advance, Maj. Gen. George G. Meade shifted his line from the north bank of the Rapidan River towards Centreville to avoid being flanked. On October 13, J.E.B. Stuart was dispatched from Warrenton towards Catlett's Station on the Orange and Alexandria Railroad to determine the location of the Union left flank.

Upon discovering the Union wagon train falling back up the railroad, Stuart determined to raid it, leaving a small detachment in his rear at Auburn. Poor scouting failed to locate the presence of a Federal column of the II and III Corps advancing on Auburn from the south. The Federal column, whose cavalry had been dispatched towards Warrenton to protect the Union left flank, stumbled into Stuart's rearguard and a small fight ensued, known as the First Battle of Auburn. The small Confederate force was quickly driven off by the superior

Union force and the Federal II Corps under Brig. Gen. Gouverneur K. Warren went in to bivouac just south Auburn, trapping Stuart's force between it and the wagon train. Stuart led his force, some 3,000 men, horses and equipment into a wooded ravine and hid from the Federals overnight. During the night Stuart dispatched a half dozen scouts in Federal uniforms through the Union lines to alert Lee, who dispatched Richard S. Ewell's Corps to Auburn to extricate Stuart at dawn the next morning.

At 3 a.m. on October 14, Warren's II Corps broke camp at Three Mile Station for Catlett's Station. At the crossing of Cedar Run just south of Auburn the ground was muddied by the passing of the Federal III Corps during the night. The wagon trains had difficulty in the mud on the slopes of the creek and accordingly Warren ordered Brig. Gen John C. Caldwell's brigade to secure the high ground north of the creek and guard the rear of the column and the wagon train as it marched to Catlett's Station. On the hill, Caldwell's men set up camp and began to make breakfast, and the Hill was soon dubbed Coffee Hill. Caldwell formed a skirmish line facing northwest towards Warrenton with the 10th New York in advance as vedettes.

Battle

At 6:15 a.m. the advance of Ewell's Corps under Maj. Gen. Robert E. Rodes's division approached the 10th New York and skirmishing broke out. The sound of gunfire carried to the ravine where Stuart was holed up and he dispatched scouts to reconnoiter the situation. Upon discovering the Federals on Coffee Hill, Stuart ordered Maj. Robert Beckham's Horse Artillery on a hill to the east of Coffee Hill. The Confederates opened a barrage on the Federals, catching them by surprise. Caldwell turned his batteries on Coffee Hill to face Beckham's, moved his line to the western slope of the hill protecting them against the artillery fire and then dispatched Brig. Gen. Alexander Hays's division against Beckham.

To protect Beckham as he limbered his guns to withdrawal, Stuart sent Brig. Gen. James B. Gordon to charge the Federal advance being led by the 125th New York. The charge temporarily stopped the advance and general skirmishing between the sides ensued. Stuart ordered Gordon to charge again to provide cover for his cavalry to escape to the southeast. Gordon fell wounded in the charge but Stuart made his escape and looped around the Federal position, joining with Maj. Gen. Jubal A. Early and Brig. Gen. Fitzhugh Lee posted to the southwest of Auburn.

With Stuart's command gone, the battle intensified along Ewell's front. Rodes advanced on Coffee Hill and Caldwell repositioned his artillery back to the west to check the Confederate advance. Rodes pressed the attack from 8 to 9 a.m.

with Early and Fitzhugh Lee's divisions joining the fray from the southwest. By 10 a.m. the fight had stalled and an hour-long artillery duel ensued until the Federal column had passed safely to Catlett's Station. Caldwell withdrew to the east pressed for a short time by Rodes. By 1 p.m. all fighting had ceased and Ewell withdrew.

Aftermath

The morning-long fight resulted in just over 100 total casualties. Strategically the result was a draw. The Confederates were able to save Stuart's command from near certain capture while the Federals were able to protect their vulnerable wagon trains. Determined to press the rear of the Union retrograde, Robert E. Lee ordered Lt. Gen. A.P. Hill to pursue the Federals east along the railroad, resulting in the Battle of Bristoe Station later that afternoon.

References

- Salmon, John S., *The Official Virginia Civil War Battlefield Guide*, Stackpole Books, 2001, ISBN 0-8117-2868-4, pp. 230–33.

External links

- National Park Service battle description[99]
- CWSAC Report Update[100]

Battle of Bristoe Station

Battle of Bristoe Station	
Part of the American Civil War	
Date	October 14, 1863
Location	Prince William County, Virginia 38.7234°N 77.5418°W[101]Coordinates: 38.7234°N 77.5418°W[101]
Result	Union victory
Belligerents	
▦ United States	▪ Confederate States
Commanders and leaders	
Gouverneur K. Warren	A.P. Hill
Units involved	
II Corps, Army of the Potomac	Third Corps, Army of Northern Virginia
Strength	
8,383	17,218
Casualties and losses	
540[102]	1,380

The **Battle of Bristoe Station** was fought on October 14, 1863, at Bristoe Station, Virginia, between Union forces under Maj. Gen. Gouverneur K. Warren and Confederate forces under Lt. Gen. A.P. Hill during the Bristoe Campaign of the American Civil War. The Union II Corps under Warren was able to surprise and repel the Confederate attack by Hill on the Union rearguard, resulting in a Union victory.

Background

The Union army was led by Maj. Gen. George G. Meade, the Confederates by General Robert E. Lee. Lee had stolen a march, passing around Cedar Mountain, the site of a battle in 1862. This forced Meade to retreat toward Centreville.[103] By withdrawing, Meade prevented Lee from falling on an exposed flank of the Army of the Potomac. Maj. Gen. Gouverneur K. Warren, commanding II Corps in Maj. Gen. Winfield S. Hancock's absence, was following V Corps on this retreat. On October 13, the II Corps had an encounter with Maj. Gen. J.E.B. Stuart's cavalry near Auburn, Virginia, the First Battle of Auburn, nicknamed "Coffee Hill." (Confederate shells interrupted Federals who were boiling coffee.) Warren had to push Stuart aside and, at the same time, retreat before the advance of the Confederate corps of Lt. Gen. Richard S. Ewell.[104] On October 14, as Warren moved toward Bristoe Station, Stuart's cavalry harassed the rear guard at the Second Battle of Auburn.

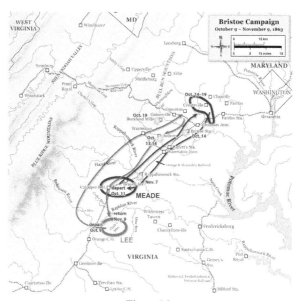

Figure 16:
Bristoe Campaign
Confederate
Union

Lt. Gen. A.P. Hill, leading the Confederate Third Corps, was advancing on Ewell's left. He reached Bristoe Station on October 14. (The town is variously called Bristoe, Bristow, and Bristo in contemporary newspapers.) Hill tried to harass the rearguard of V Corps just across Broad Run, but he missed the presence of II Corps just coming up from Auburn.[105] Seeing Heth's advance, Warren rapidly deployed his forces behind an embankment of the Orange and Alexandria Railroad near Bristoe Station. The result was a powerful ambush as Hill's corps moved to attack the Federal rear guard across Broad Run.[106]

Battle

Maj. Gen. Henry Heth's division moved to attack the V Corps, but it was redirected to attack the II Corps. Union artillery, including the battery of Capt. R. Bruce Ricketts, opened on the Confederates; and infantry fire soon was added.[107] Despite this fire, Heth's men briefly secured a foothold in the lines of Col. James E. Mallon in the second division under Brig. Gen. Alexander S. Webb. The Confederates were driven back, and five guns of a Confederate battery were captured in a Federal counterattack. Col. Mallon was killed in

Figure 17: *Park at the site of the battle*

the fighting. The Confederate division of Maj. Gen. Richard H. Anderson attacked the lines of Brig. Gen. Alexander Hays's division and also was repelled. Brig. Gen. Carnot Posey was mortally wounded in that attack. Two of Heth's brigade commanders, William Whedbee Kirkland and John Rogers Cooke, also were badly wounded.[108]

Aftermath

Union casualties were 540, Confederate about 1,380. Warren, seeing Lt. Gen. Richard S. Ewell's Second Corps coming up on his left, eventually had to withdraw.[109] Lee is said to have cut off Hill's excuses for this defeat by saying, "Well, well, general, bury these poor men and let us say no more about it."[110] The Union forces won the battle, but they had to retreat to Centreville, Virginia, before standing their ground. When they pulled back, starting on October 18, the Confederates destroyed much of the Orange and Alexandria Railroad. Meade had to rebuild the railroad when he reoccupied the area around Bristoe Station. Warren won such reputation as a corps commander that he was given V Corps as a regular assignment after Hancock returned to the Army of the Potomac in 1864.

References

- National Park Service battle description[111]
- CWSAC Report Update[112]
- Freeman, Douglas S. *Lee's Lieutenants: A Study in Command*. 3 vols. New York: Scribner, 1946. ISBN 0-684-85979-3.
- Jordan, David M. *Happiness Is Not My Companion: The Life of General G. K. Warren*. Bloomington: Indiana University Press, 2001. ISBN 0-253-33904-9.
- Walker, Francis A. *History of the Second Army Corps in the Army of the Potomac*[113]. New York: C. Scribner's Sons, 1886. OCLC 287902026[114].

Further reading

- Henderson, William D. *The Road to Bristoe Station: Campaigning with Lee and Meade, August 1–October 20, 1863*. Lynchburg, VA: H. E. Howard, 1987. ISBN 978-0-930919-45-0.
- Tighe, Adrian G. *The Bristoe Campaign: General Lee's Last Strategic Offensive with the Army of Northern Virginia, October 1863*. Xlibris, 2011. ISBN 978-1-4568-8869-5.

External links

- Battle of Bristoe Station in *Encyclopedia Virginia*[115]
- Prince William County Historic Preservation / Bristoe Station Battlefield[116]
- "To Halt Was to Await Annihilation – Lee Lets Meade Slip Away, October 14, 1863"[117]. Civil War Daily Gazette. Retrieved 7 August 2016.
- Alexander, Edward S (October 14, 2013). "Swapped Identities: Battle of Bristoe Station, October 14, 1863"[118]. Emerging Civil War Blog. Retrieved 7 August 2016.
- Campi, Jim. "A Roar From The Portals of Hell: A.P. Hill Stumbles Into Tragedy At Bristoe Station"[119]. Civil War Trust. Retrieved 7 August 2016.

Battle of Buckland Mills

Battle of Buckland Mills	
Part of American Civil War	
Date	October 19, 1863
Location	Fauquier County, Virginia
Result	Confederate victory
Belligerents	
≡ United States (Union)	▣ CSA (Confederacy)
Commanders and leaders	
Hugh Judson Kilpatrick	J.E.B. Stuart
Casualties and losses	
230	

The **Battle of Buckland Mills**, also known as **The Buckland Races** or **Chestnut Hill**, was fought on October 19, 1863, between Union and Confederate forces in the American Civil War. Union cavalry led by Brig. Gen. Judson Kilpatrick were caught in a Confederate ambush and defeated.

Near Buckland Mills, on Broad Run, Confederate cavalry commander Maj. Gen. J.E.B. Stuart, with Maj. Gen. Wade Hampton's cavalry division, were covering Gen. Robert E. Lee's retirement from his defeat at Bristoe to the Rappahannock River. On October 19, they turned on Kilpatrick's pursuing Federal cavalry, while Maj. Gen. Fitzhugh Lee's division charged the Federal flank. Kilpatrick was routed, fleeing five miles to Haymarket and Gainesville. The Confederates derisively called the affair "The Buckland Races", although some Confederate commanders likened it to a fox hunt.

References

- Adams, James Truslow, *Dictionary of American History*, New York: Charles Scribner's Sons, 1940.
- National Park Service battle description[120]
- CWSAC Report Update and Resurvey: Individual Battlefield Profiles[121]

Coordinates: 38.7747°N 77.692°W[122]

Second Battle of Rappahannock Station

Second Battle of Rappahannock Station	
Part of the American Civil War	
Date	November 7, 1863
Location	Culpeper County and Fauquier County, Virginia
Result	Union victory
Belligerents	
United States (Union)	CSA (Confederacy)
Commanders and leaders	
George G. Meade	Robert E. Lee
Strength	
2,000	2,000
Casualties and losses	
419 (Killed, wounded or captured)	1,670 (Approx 1,600 captured)

The **Second Battle of Rappahannock Station** took place on November 7, 1863, near the village of Rappahannock Station (now Remington, Virginia), on the Orange and Alexandria Railroad, between Confederate forces under Maj. Gen. Jubal Early and Union forces under Maj. Gen. John Sedgwick as part of the Bristoe Campaign of the American Civil War. The battle resulted in a victory for the Union.

Background

After the Battle of Gettysburg in July 1863, the Union and Confederate armies drifted south and for three months sparred with one another on the rolling plains of northern Virginia. Little was accomplished, however, and in late October General Robert E. Lee withdrew his Confederate army behind the Rappahannock River, a line he hoped to maintain throughout the winter.

A single pontoon bridge at the town of Rappahannock Station was the only connection Lee retained with the northern bank of the river. The bridge was protected by a bridgehead on the north bank consisting on two redoubts and connecting trenches. Confederate batteries posted on hills south of the river gave additional strength to the position.

The bridgehead was an integral part of Lee's strategy to defend the Rappahannock River line. As he later explained, by holding the bridgehead he could "threaten any flank movement the enemy might make above or below, and thus compel him to divide his forces, when it was hoped that an opportunity would be presented to concentrate on one or the other part." The Union Army of the Potomac's commander, Maj. Gen. George G. Meade, divided his forces just as Lee expected. He ordered Maj. Gen. John Sedgwick to attack the Confederate position at Rappahannock Station while Maj. Gen. William H. French forced a crossing five miles downstream at Kelly's Ford. Once both Sedgwick and French were safely across the river, the reunited army would proceed to Brandy Station.

Battle

The operation went according to plan. Shortly after noon on November 7, French drove back Confederate defenders at Kelly's Ford and crossed the river. As he did so, Sedgwick advanced toward Rappahannock Station. Lee learned of these developments sometime after noon and immediately put his troops in motion to meet the enemy. His plan was to resist Sedgwick with a small force at Rappahannock Station while attacking French at Kelly's Ford with the larger part of his army. The success of the plan depended on his ability to maintain the Rappahannock Station bridgehead until French was defeated.

Sedgwick first engaged the Confederates at 3 p.m. when Maj. Gen. Albion P. Howe's division of the VI Corps drove in Confederate skirmishers and seized a range of high ground three-quarters of a mile from the river. Howe placed Union batteries on these hills that pounded the enemy earthworks with a "rapid and vigorous" fire. Confederate guns across the river returned the fire, but with little effect.

Maj. Gen. Jubal Early's division occupied the bridgehead defenses that day. Early posted Brig. Gen. Harry T. Hays's Louisiana brigade and Captain Charles A. Green's four gun Louisiana Guard Artillery in the works and at 4:30 p.m. reinforced them with three North Carolina regiments led by Colonel Archibald Godwin. The addition of Godwin's troops increased the number of Confederate defenders at the bridgehead to nearly 2,000.

Sedgwick continued shelling the Confederates throughout the late afternoon, but otherwise he showed no disposition to attack. As the day drew to a close, Lee became convinced that the movement against the bridgehead was merely a feint to cover French's crossing farther downstream. He was mistaken. At dusk the shelling stopped, and Sedgwick's infantry rushed suddenly upon the works. Col. Peter Ellmaker's brigade advanced adjacent to the railroad, preceded by skirmishers of the 6th Maine Infantry. No Union regiment gained more laurels that day nor suffered higher casualties. At the command "Forward, double-quick!" they surged over the Confederate works and engaged Hays's men in hand-to-hand combat. Without assistance, the 6th Maine breached the Confederate line and planted its flags on the parapet of the easternmost redoubt. Moments later the 5th Wisconsin swarmed over the walls of the western redoubt, likewise wresting it from Confederate control.

On the right, Union forces achieved comparable success. Just minutes after Ellmaker's brigade penetrated Hays's line, Col. Emory Upton's brigade overran Godwin's position. Upton reformed his lines inside the Confederate works and sent a portion of the 121st New York to seize the pontoon bridge, while the rest of his command wheeled right to attack the confused Confederate horde now massed at the lower end of the bridgehead.

Confederate resistance dissolved as hundreds of soldiers threw down their arms and surrendered. Others sought to gain the opposite shore by swimming the icy river or by running the gauntlet of Union rifle fire at the bridge. Confederate troops south of the Rappahannock looked on hopelessly as Union soldiers herded their comrades to the rear as prisoners of war.

Aftermath

In all, 1,670 Confederates were killed, wounded, or captured in the brief struggle, more than eighty percent of those engaged. Union casualty figures, by contrast, were small: 419 in all.

For the North the battle had been "a complete and glorious victory," an engagement "as short as it was decisive," reflecting "infinite credit upon all concerned."[123] Maj. Gen. Horatio G. Wright noted that it was the first instance in which Union troops had carried a strongly entrenched Confederate position in the first assault. Brig. Gen. Harry Hays claimed to have been attacked by no less than 20,000 to 25,000 Union soldiers—a figure ten times the actual number.

The battle had been as humiliating for the South as it had been glorious for the North. Two of the Confederacy's finest brigades, sheltered behind entrenchments and well supported by artillery, had been routed and captured by an enemy force of equal size. Col. Walter H. Taylor of Lee's staff called it, "the saddest chapter in the history of this army," the result of "miserable, miserable management." An enlisted soldier put it more plainly. "I don't know much about it," he said, "but it seems to be that our army was surprised."

Lee would later call on subordinates to submit reports on the battle in an effort to determine what had gone wrong, but on the night of November 7 more pressing matters demanded his attention. Loss of the bridgehead destroyed his plans for an offensive and left his army dangerously extended on a now indefensible front. Meade, acting quickly, might pin Lee's army against the

Rapidan River just as Lee had tried to pin Maj. Gen. John Pope's army against the Rappahannock River one year earlier in the Second Battle of Bull Run. Lee immediately canceled his plans for an attack on French and within hours had his army marching south.

Notes

References

- Brochure[124] by the National Park Service
- National Park Service battle description[125]
- CWSAC Report Update[126]

Coordinates: 38.5330°N 77.8136°W[127]

Battle of Mine Run

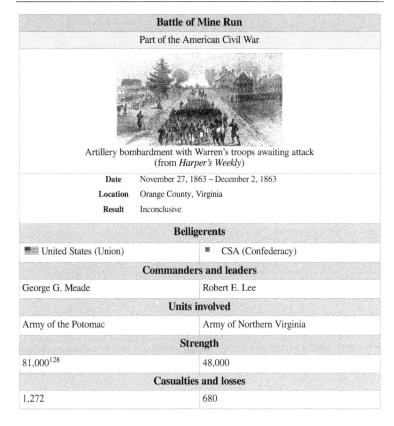

Battle of Mine Run	
Part of the American Civil War	
Artillery bombardment with Warren's troops awaiting attack (from *Harper's Weekly*)	
Date	November 27, 1863 – December 2, 1863
Location	Orange County, Virginia
Result	Inconclusive
Belligerents	
United States (Union)	CSA (Confederacy)
Commanders and leaders	
George G. Meade	Robert E. Lee
Units involved	
Army of the Potomac	Army of Northern Virginia
Strength	
81,000[128]	48,000
Casualties and losses	
1,272	680

The **Battle of Mine Run**, also known as **Payne's Farm**, or **New Hope Church**, or the **Mine Run Campaign** (November 27 – December 2, 1863), was conducted in Orange County, Virginia, in the American Civil War.

An unsuccessful attempt of the Union Army of the Potomac to defeat the Confederate Army of Northern Virginia, it was marked by false starts and low casualties and ended hostilities in the Eastern Theater for the year.

Background

After the Battle of Gettysburg in July, Confederate Gen. Robert E. Lee and his command retreated back across the Potomac River into Virginia. Union commander Maj. Gen. George G. Meade was widely criticized for failing to pursue aggressively and defeat Lee's army. Meade planned new offensives in

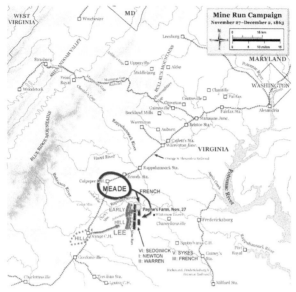

Figure 18:
Mine Run Campaign
Confederate
Union

Figure 19: *Troops crossing at Germanna Ford during the Mine Run campaign (from Harper's Weekly)*

Virginia for the fall. His first attempt was a series of inconclusive duels and maneuvers in October and November known as the Bristoe Campaign.

In late November, Meade attempted to steal a march through the Wilderness of Spotsylvania and strike the right flank of the Confederate Army south of the Rapidan River. Meade had intelligence reports that Lee's army, half the size of Meade's Army of the Potomac (actually 48,000 to Meade's 81,000), was split in two, separated by Clark's Mountain, with the two flanks anchored at Mine Run and Liberty Mills, over thirty miles apart. His plan was to cross the Rapidan at points beyond Maj. Gen. J.E.B. Stuart's cavalry screen, overwhelm the right flank (Lt. Gen. Richard S. Ewell's Second Corps) and then follow up with the remainder (Lt. Gen. A.P. Hill's Third Corps).[129]

Unlike Maj. Gen. Joseph Hooker's plan in the Chancellorsville Campaign earlier that year on essentially the same ground, Meade planned no diversions; he intended a lightning strike with his entire army. The army marched on November 25 and got off to a good start, aided by fog on Clark's Mountain, which screened his movements from Confederate lookouts. However, Maj. Gen. William H. French's III Corps got bogged down in fording the river at Jacob's Ford, causing traffic jams when they moved their artillery to Germanna Ford, where other units were attempting to cross.

Opposing forces
Battle

Speed had escaped Meade, who was furious with French, and this allowed Lee time to react. Lee ordered Maj. Gen. Jubal A. Early, in temporary command of Ewell's Second Corps, to march east on the Orange Turnpike to meet French's advance near Payne's Farm. Brig. Gen. Joseph B. Carr's division of French's corps attacked twice. Maj. Gen. Edward "Allegheny" Johnson's division counterattacked, but was scattered by heavy fire and broken terrain.

After dark, Lee withdrew to prepared field fortifications along Mine Run. The next day the Union Army closed on the Confederate position. Meade planned a heavy artillery bombardment followed by Maj. Gen. Gouverneur K. Warren's II Corps attack in the south, then Maj. Gen. John Sedgwick's VI Corps in the north an hour later. Lee planned an assault for December 2 that would have exploited the dangling left flank of the Union line, discovered the previous day by Maj. Gen. Wade Hampton's cavalry. Although the Union bombardment began on schedule, the major attack did not materialize; Meade concluded that the Confederate line was too strong to attack (although Warren is credited with getting the attack canceled) and retired during the night of December 1–2, ending the fall campaign. Lee was chagrined to find he had no one left in his front to attack.

Aftermath

The Army of the Potomac went into winter quarters at Brandy Station, Virginia. Mine Run had been Meade's final opportunity to plan a strategic offensive before the arrival of Ulysses S. Grant as general-in-chief the following spring. Lee also regretted the inconclusive results. He was quoted as saying, "I am too old to command this army. We never should have permitted those people to get away." Confederate hopes of repeating their Chancellorsville triumph had been dashed. The Mine Run Campaign was Meade's last and failed attempt in 1863 to destroy Lee's Army of Northern Virginia before winter halted military operations[130]

References

- Eicher, David J. *The Longest Night: A Military History of the Civil War.* New York: Simon & Schuster, 2001. ISBN 0-684-84944-5.
- Esposito, Vincent J. *West Point Atlas of American Wars.* New York: Frederick A. Praeger, 1959. OCLC 5890637[131]. The collection of maps (without explanatory text) is available online at the West Point website[132].
- Salmon, John S. *The Official Virginia Civil War Battlefield Guide.* Mechanicsburg, PA: Stackpole Books, 2001. ISBN 0-8117-2868-4.
- National Park Service battle description[133]

Further reading

- Graham, Martin F., and George F. Skoch. *Mine Run: A Campaign of Lost Opportunities, October 21, 1863–May 1, 1864.* Lynchburg, VA: H. E. Howard, 1987. ISBN 978-0-930919-48-1.

External links

- Mine Run Campaign in *Encyclopedia Virginia*[134]

Coordinates: 38.3379°N 77.8187°W[135]

Notable individuals

William H. French

William Henry French	
General William Henry French	
Born	January 13, 1815 Baltimore, Maryland
Died	May 20, 1881 (aged 66) Washington, D.C.
Place of burial	Rock Creek Cemetery, Washington, D.C.
Allegiance	United States of America Union
Service/branch	United States Army Union Army
Years of service	1837–1880
Rank	⬛⭐⭐ Major General
Commands held	III Corps
Battles/wars	Second Seminole War Mexican-American War American Civil War

William Henry French (January 13, 1815 – May 20, 1881) was a career
United States Army officer and a Union Army General in the American Civil
War. He rose to temporarily command a corps within the Army of the Potomac, but was relieved of active field duty following poor performance by his
command during the Mine Run Campaign in late 1863. He remained in the
Army and went on to command several Army installations before his retirement in 1880.

Early life and career

William H. French was born in Baltimore, Maryland. He graduated from the
United States Military Academy in 1837 and was commissioned a second lieutenant in the 1st U.S. Artillery. He briefly served in the Second Seminole War
and was then assigned to garrison duty along the Canadian border from late
1837 through 1838, when he was reassigned to other military posts for the
next decade.

During the Mexican-American War, French was aide-de-camp to General
Franklin Pierce, and also on the staff of General Robert Patterson. He was
engaged in the siege of Vera Cruz, and received two brevet promotions for
bravery: to captain for Cerro Gordo and to major for Contreras and Churubusco.

Between 1850 and 1852, he again served against the Seminole Indians in
Florida and was the commanding officer of Stonewall Jackson. The two dis-
agreed often and French's assignment with Jackson led to the two filing numerous charges against each other with U.S. Army authorities. After Florida,
French served on frontier duty until 1861.

He was the co-author of *Instruction for Field Artillery* (1860), along with
William F. Barry and Henry J. Hunt.

Civil War

At the start of the Civil War, Captain French and the 1st U.S. Artillery were
stationed at Eagle Pass, Texas. He refused to surrender his garrison to the
Confederate-aligned state authorities as they requested. Instead, he moved his
men to the mouth of the Río Grande in sixteen days and sailed to Key West,
where he quartered at the Federal military post there. Shortly thereafter, he was
elevated to major and assumed command of the base. In conjunction with the
Union Navy, he was instrumental in shutting off Key West to slave traders.[136]

Figure 20: *Commanders of the Army of the Potomac, Gouverneur K. Warren, William H. French, George G. Meade, Henry J. Hunt, Andrew A. Humphreys and George Sykes in September 1863.*

He was promoted to brigadier general of volunteers as of September 28, 1861, and was assigned to the Army of the Potomac, where he commanded a brigade of the II Corps in the Peninsula Campaign. He was engaged at the battles of Yorktown, Seven Pines, Oak Grove, Gaines' Mill, Garnett's & Golding's Farm, Savage's Station, Glendale, and Malvern Hill. French received praise in official reports for his actions and leadership, and was promoted to command a division during the Northern Virginia Campaign.

French commanded the 3rd Division of the II Corps at the Battle of Antietam, making the first attack on the Confederate Division in the Sunken Road. He was promoted to major general on November 29, 1862. He led his division in the battles of Fredericksburg and Chancellorsville.

French commanded elements of the VIII Corps and the District of Harpers Ferry during the Gettysburg Campaign, but shortly after Maj. Gen. Daniel E. Sickles was wounded at the Battle of Gettysburg, French assumed command of the battered III Corps. His military reputation was ruined during the Mine Run Campaign in November 1863 when Maj. Gen. George G. Meade claimed that French's corps moved too slowly to exploit a potential advantage over Gen. Robert E. Lee. This engagement was the last for the III Corps, which was

Figure 21: *General William H. French and staff in September 1863.*

reorganized out of the Union Army in the spring of 1864, and French was mustered out of volunteer service on May 6, 1864.

He remained in the regular army, and for the remainder of the war, he served on military boards in Washington, D.C.. French ended the war with the regular army rank of colonel of the 4th U.S. Artillery.

Postbellum career

Following the war, French commanded the 2nd Artillery on the Pacific Coast from 1865 until 1872, including an assignment as commander of Fort Mc-Dowell in San Francisco Bay. In 1875, he was appointed the commander of Fort McHenry near Baltimore. In July 1880, at his own request, being over sixty-two years of age, he was retired.

French died in Washington, D.C., and is buried there in Rock Creek Cemetery.

Family

He married Caroline Read (1820 - 1884). They had five children: Frank French (1842 - 1865), Anna French Clem (1852 - 1899), Frederick French

(1855 - 1906), George French (1857 - 1895), and Rosalie French Conklin (1861 - 1891).

His grandson, John French Conklin (1891–1973), was also a graduate of the U.S. Military Academy and a brigadier general in the United States Army.[137]

References

- Eicher, John H., and David J. Eicher. *Civil War High Commands*. Stanford, CA: Stanford University Press, 2001. ISBN 0-8047-3641-3.
- Warner, Ezra J. *Generals in Blue: Lives of the Union Commanders*. Baton Rouge: Louisiana State University Press, 1964. ISBN 0-8071-0822-7.

Attribution:

- ⊚ This article incorporates text from a publication now in the public domain: Wilson, James Grant; Fiske, John, eds. (1891). "article name needed". *Appletons' Cyclopædia of American Biography*. New York: D. Appleton.

External links

- Photo gallery of General French[138] at the Wayback Machine (archived February 8, 2008)

Military offices		
Preceded by **David B. Birney**	**Commander of the III Corps (Army of the Potomac)** July 7, 1863 – January 28, 1864	Succeeded by **David B. Birney**
Preceded by **David B. Birney**	**Commander of the III Corps (Army of the Potomac)** February 17, 1864 – March 24, 1864	Succeeded by **Command absorbed into II Corps (Army of the Potomac) and VI Corps (Army of the Potomac)**

John D. Imboden

John D. Imboden	
	John Daniel Imboden photo taken in the 1860s
Born	February 16, 1823 Staunton, Virginia
Died	August 15, 1895 (aged 72) Damascus, Virginia
Place of burial	Hollywood Cemetery, Richmond, Virginia
Allegiance	Confederate States of America
Service/-branch	Confederate States Army
Years of service	1861–1865
Rank	Brigadier General
Battles/wars	American Civil War • First Battle of Manassas • Gettysburg Campaign • Valley Campaigns of 1864
Other work	lawyer, writer

John Daniel Imboden (/ɪmˈboʊdɛn/; February 16, 1823 – August 15, 1895), American lawyer, Virginia state legislator and a Confederate army general. During the American Civil War, he commanded an irregular cavalry force. After the war, he resumed practicing law, became a writer, and was active in land development founding the town of Damascus, Virginia.

Figure 22: *John Daniel Imboden in military uniform*

Early life and career

Imboden was born near Staunton, Virginia, in the Shenandoah Valley to George William Imboden (1793-1875) and Isabella Wunderlich who had eleven children. His father participated in the War of 1812. Imboden started his education in a county school, then in 1841-1842 he attended Washington College. He found employment as a teacher at the Virginia School for the Deaf and the Blind in Staunton. Later, he studied law, was admitted to the Virginia bar, and entered into partnership with William Frazier to create a law firm. In December 1844, Imboden became a member of the Staunton Masonic lodge, Number 13, Ancient Free and Accepted Masons (A.F. & A.M.).[6] He enrolled in Virginia's militia and was among founders of the Staunton Light Artillery. Despite having no military training, Imboden received a commission as captain in the Staunton Artillery of the Virginia State Militia on November 28, 1859. As an advocate of state rights, Imboden was twice elected to the House of Delegates of the Virginia General Assembly.[139]

Civil War service

On July 1, 1861, Staunton Light Artillery, with its four bronze, 6-pounder guns and 107 officers and men, was mustered in the Confederate States Army.[140,141] Imboden commanded the unit during the capture of Harpers Ferry. While commanding his artillery battery at the First Battle of Bull Run, Imboden perforated his left eardrum firing an artillery piece, causing subsequent deafness in that ear. On September 9, 1862, Imboden left the artillery to recruit a battalion of partisan rangers and was promoted to colonel of the 62nd Virginia Mounted Infantry (1st Partisan Rangers). He fought with Maj. Gen. Thomas J. "Stonewall" Jackson in the Valley Campaign at Cross Keys and Port Republic. He was promoted to brigadier general on January 28, 1863.[142]

Along with Brig. Gen. William E. "Grumble" Jones, Imboden led the famous Jones-Imboden Raid of 3,400 partisan rangers into northwestern Virginia, destroying rail track and bridges of the Baltimore and Ohio Railroad. During the raid he also captured thousands of horses and heads of cattle and ruined the petroleum fields in the Kanawha Valley. This raid covered 400 miles (640 km) in 37 days. In the Gettysburg Campaign, Imboden's brigade served under Maj. Gen. J.E.B. Stuart as the rearguard for Gen. Robert E. Lee's movement north through the Shenandoah Valley. (His brigade did not participate in Stuart's foray away from Lee's army, but instead raided the Baltimore and Ohio Railroad between Martinsburg, West Virginia, and Cumberland, Maryland.)

During the Battle of Gettysburg, Imboden's men stayed in the rear and guarded ammunition and supply trains in Chambersburg, Pennsylvania. During the Confederate retreat, Imboden was in charge of escorting the wagon trains of thousands of wounded soldiers back to Virginia. On July 6, 1863, the Potomac River was flooding at Williamsport, Maryland, and Imboden's wagon train was trapped. He put together a defensive force that included an artillery battery and as many of the wounded who could operate muskets. This hastily organized force turned back attacks from Union cavalry generals John Buford and Judson Kilpatrick, saving the wagon train. Robert E. Lee praised Imboden for the way in which he "gallantly repulsed" the Union cavalry.

Returning to the Shenandoah Valley, Imboden responded to a request from General Lee to distract the enemy in his front by leading a raid on the vulnerable Union detachment at Charles Town, West Virginia, on October 18, 1863 at the Battle of Charlestown. Imboden reported,

The surprise was complete, the enemy having no suspicion of our approach until I had the town entirely surrounded. ... To my demand for a surrender Colonel Simpson requested an hour for consideration. I offered him five minutes, to which he replied, 'Take us if you can'. I immediately opened on the buildings with artillery at less than 200 yards, and with half a dozen

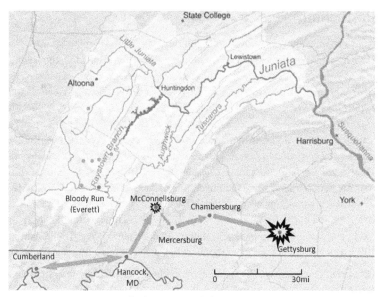

Figure 23: *Imboden's actions before Battle of Gettysburg*

shells drove out the enemy into the streets, when he formed and fled toward Harper's Ferry.

Union Brig. Gen. Jeremiah Cutler Sullivan soon sent a rescue column from nearby Harpers Ferry and drove Imboden back up the valley. Sullivan reported, "The cavalry came up with the enemy this side of Charlestown, and drove them through the town. Artillery coming up, drove them about 4 miles. A portion of infantry force..., reaching them, the enemy were driven from every position they took, to near Berryville."

Imboden and John C. Breckinridge's forces defeated Union Maj. Gen. Franz Sigel's command at the Battle of New Market on May 15, 1864. He returned to Virginia and commanded a brigade in Maj. Gen. Robert Ransom's cavalry division of the Second Corps of the Army of Northern Virginia under Lt. Gen. Jubal A. Early in the Valley Campaigns of 1864. He was incapacitated by typhoid fever and left the active cavalry service.

Beginning on January 2, 1865, Imboden commanded Camp Millen, Georgia, then the prison camp at Aiken, South Carolina as well as other prison camps in Georgia, Alabama, and Mississippi throughout 1865 until the end of the war. He was paroled in Augusta, Georgia on May 3 of that year.

Postbellum

After the war, Imboden moved to Richmond, Virginia, where he resumed his work as a lawyer, serving first in Richmond and then in Abingdon, the county seat of Washington County. He published several articles and books about the Civil War, and also contributed to *The War of the Rebellion: A Compilation of the Official Records of the Union and Confederate Armies (128 vols., 1880-1901).*[143] Imboden became a vocal advocate of the development of Virginia's natural resources and transportation infrastructure. He published in 1872 a pamphlet, *The Coal and Iron Resources of Virginia: Their Extent, Commercial Value, and Early Development Considered.*[144] Around 1875, he moved to southwestern Virginia where he hoped to mine coal and iron ore deposits. He founded a town of Damascus, Virginia, which became a lumber center in the late 19th and early 20th century.[145] In 1876, he became a commissioner of the Centennial International Exposition in Philadelphia, Pennsylvania, and in 1893, he was a commissioner of the World's Columbian Exposition in Chicago.

He died in Damascus in 1895, and is buried in the *Generals section* of Hollywood Cemetery in Richmond, Virginia.[146,147]

Family

During his life, Imboden was married five times; five out of his nine children were alive at the time of his death in 1895.[148] On June 16, 1845, Imboden married Eliza "Dice" Allen McCue, who was a daughter of Colonel Franklin McCue. The Imbodens built a house in Staunton which they called the "Ingleside Cottage". They had four children, one died before reaching three years. On December 23, 1857, his wife of twelve years died. On May 12, 1859, Imboden married Mary Wilson McPhail, who gave birth to three children.[149] Later, he married Edna Porter, then Anna Lockett, and finally Florence Crockett.

Works

- Imboden, John D. *Organized and Authorized Partisan Rangers.* Staunton, Va., 1862. (Recruiting pamphlet)
- Imboden, John D. *Virginia, the Home for the Northern Farmer: Three Letters from Gen. J.d. Imboden, Domestic Agent of Immigration for the State of Virginia, to Hon. Horace Greeley.* New York: D. Taylor, 1869.
- Imboden, John D. *Lee at Gettysburg.* New York, 1871.
- Imboden, John D. *Reminiscences of Lee and Jackson.* New York, 1871.

- Imboden, John D. *The Coal and Iron Resources of Virginia: Their Extent, Commercial Value, and Early Development Considered. a Paper Read Before a Meeting of Members of the Legislature and Prominent Citizens in the Capitol at Richmond, February 19th, 1872.* Richmond: Clemmitt & Jones, printers, 1872.
- Imboden, John D. *Important to All Interested in Virginia, U.S.* London: Foreign and Colonial Estates Exchange Agency, 1873.
- Imboden, John D. Jackson at Harper's Ferry in 1861. In *Battles and Leaders of the Civil War,* ed. by Robert U. Johnson and Clarence C. Buel (1884-1887). **1.1** (1884): 111-125.
- Imboden, John D. *Coal and Coke: Coal Interests of South Western Virginia.* s.l., 1894.

Further reading

- Brown, Kent Masterson. *Retreat from Gettysburg: Lee, Logistics, & the Pennsylvania Campaign.* Chapel Hill: University of North Carolina Press, 2005. ISBN 0-8078-2921-8.
- Eicher, John H., and David J. Eicher, *Civil War High Commands.* Stanford: Stanford University Press, 2001. ISBN 978-0-8047-3641-1.
- Sifakis, Stewart. *Who Was Who in the Civil War.* New York: Facts On File, 1988. ISBN 978-0-8160-1055-4.
- Tucker, Spencer. *Brigadier General John D. Imboden: Confederate Commander in the Shenandoah.*[150] Lexington: University Press of Kentucky, 2003. ISBN 978-0-8131-2266-3.
- Warner, Ezra J. *Generals in Gray: Lives of the Confederate Commanders.* Baton Rouge: Louisiana State University Press, 1959. ISBN 978-0-8071-0823-9.
- Wittenberg, Eric J., J. David Petruzzi, and Michael F. Nugent. *One Continuous Fight: The Retreat from Gettysburg and the Pursuit of Lee's Army of Northern Virginia, July 4–14, 1863.* New York: Savas Beatie, 2008. ISBN 978-1-932714-43-2.

External links

 Wikimedia Commons has media related to *John Daniel Imboden*.

- John D. Imboden[151] at *Find a Grave*
- John D. Imboden[152]

William E. Jones

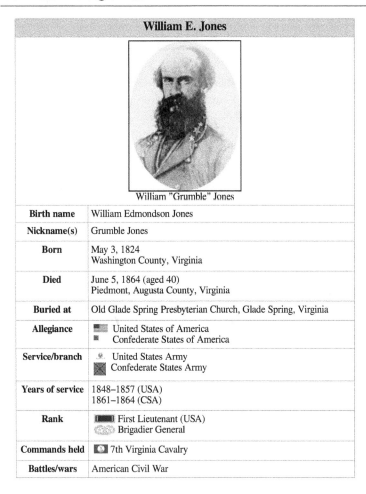

William E. Jones	
Birth name	William Edmondson Jones
Nickname(s)	Grumble Jones
Born	May 3, 1824 Washington County, Virginia
Died	June 5, 1864 (aged 40) Piedmont, Augusta County, Virginia
Buried at	Old Glade Spring Presbyterian Church, Glade Spring, Virginia
Allegiance	United States of America Confederate States of America
Service/branch	United States Army Confederate States Army
Years of service	1848–1857 (USA) 1861–1864 (CSA)
Rank	First Lieutenant (USA) Brigadier General
Commands held	7th Virginia Cavalry
Battles/wars	American Civil War

Caption within image: William "Grumble" Jones

William Edmondson "Grumble" Jones (May 3, 1824 – June 5, 1864) was a planter, a career United States Army officer, and a Confederate cavalry General, killed in the Battle of Piedmont in the American Civil War.

Early life

Jones was born in Washington County, Virginia. After graduating from Emory and Henry College in Virginia in 1844, he graduated from the United States Military Academy in 1848, ranking twelfth out of 48 cadets, and was commissioned a brevet Second Lieutenant in the U.S. Mounted Rifles. He served with the cavalry fighting Indians in the west and was promoted to First Lieutenant in 1854. His nickname, "Grumble", reflects his irritable disposition, undoubtedly exacerbated by the death of his wife, who was washed from his arms in a shipwreck shortly after their marriage in 1852 while en route to Texas. He resigned his commission in 1857, and became a farmer near Glade Spring, Virginia.

Civil War

At the start of the Civil War, Jones joined the 1st Virginia Cavalry Regiment as a Captain, commanding a company he had raised. On May 9 he was promoted to Major in Virginia's Provisional Army, and later that month both Jones and the regiment were transferred into the Confederate Army. Jones served under Col. J.E.B. Stuart in the First Battle of Bull Run in July 1861. The following month he was promoted to the rank of Colonel was given command of the 1st Virginia Cavalry.[153]

In the fall of 1861 the Confederate forces underwent a massive reorganization, during which the enlisted men could elect their officers. As a result, Jones was not re-elected to his post as commander of the 1st Virginia Cavalry. That September he was appointed to command the 7th Virginia Cavalry. He led the regiment into Western Virginia, along the Potomac River. In March 1862 Jones was given command of all cavalry in the Valley District.[154]

Returning to eastern Virginia, Jones's cavalry was distinguished in the Second Bull Run Campaign; he was wounded in a skirmish at Orange Court House on August 2. He was part of Stuart's ostentatious raid around Maj. Gen. George B. McClellan's army preceding the Seven Days battles. He was promoted to Brigadier General on September 19, 1862, and on November 8, was assigned to command the 4th Brigade of Stuart's Cavalry Division in the Army of Northern Virginia. This brigade was known as Robertson's, or the "Laurel brigade," and consisted entirely of Virginians, formerly commanded by Turner Ashby. Based

Figure 24: *Confederate Cavalry General William E. Jones photographed while still a colonel with the 7th Virginia Cavalry in 1862.*

on the request of Lt. Gen. Thomas J. "Stonewall" Jackson, on December 29, 1862, he assumed command of the Valley District.

In the spring of 1863, Jones and Brig. Gen. John D. Imboden raided the Baltimore and Ohio Railroad west of Cumberland, Maryland, destroying much of the railroad and public property in the area, including the Burning Springs Complex on May 9, 1863. Rejoining Stuart, he fought in the largest cavalry engagement of the war, the Battle of Brandy Station, June 9, 1863, at the start of the Gettysburg Campaign. He was surprised, as was all of Stuart's command, to be hit out of blue by Union cavalry under Maj. Gen. Alfred Pleasonton. Jones's brigade was outnumbered by the division of his West Point classmate, Brig. Gen. John Buford, but it held its own and ended the fight with more horses and more and better small-arms than at the beginning, capturing two regimental colors, an artillery battery, and about 250 prisoners.

As the Gettysburg Campaign continued, Jones screened the Army of Northern Virginia's rear guard during the advance north through the Shenandoah Valley, by holding gaps in the mountains that separated them from Union observation and interference. As the Battle of Gettysburg commenced on July 1, 1863, Jones' brigade crossed the Potomac River at Williamsport, Maryland, but stayed away from the principal battlefield, guarding the trains and Harpers

Ferry. Jones was disgruntled that Stuart had not taken him on his movement around the Union flank to join up with General Richard S. Ewell's Second Corps on the Susquehanna River. Before moving into Pennsylvania, General Robert E. Lee ordered Ewell to capture Harrisburg if practicable. The disagreeable Jones often clashed with Stuart. On July 3, Jones's brigade fought a sharp battle with the 6th U.S. Cavalry at Fairfield, Pennsylvania, then again at Funkstown, Maryland, a few days later. After Lee's army completed its retreat back to Virginia, Jones's men fought twice again with Buford at Brandy Station, on August 1 and October 10, 1863.

In October, Stuart's dissatisfaction with Jones reached a boil and he court-martialed Jones for insulting him. Although Grumble was found guilty, Robert E. Lee intervened, and he was transferred to the Trans-Allegheny Department in West Virginia. Jones recruited a brigade of cavalry there and campaigned in eastern Tennessee with Lt. Gen. James Longstreet's forces during the winter and spring of 1864. In May, Jones assumed command of the Confederate forces in the Shenandoah Valley who were defending against the halting advance of Maj. Gen. David Hunter towards Lynchburg, Virginia, in the Valley Campaigns of 1864. In the Battle of Piedmont on June 5, 1864, Jones was shot in the head and killed while leading a charge against a superior attacking force.

Grumble Jones is buried in the Old Glade Spring Presbyterian Church graveyard, Glade Spring, Virginia. His fellow cavalry general, Brig. Gen. Imboden, wrote that Jones

... was an old army officer, brave as a lion and had seen much service, and was known as a hard fighter. He was a man, however, of high temper, morose and fretful. He held the fighting qualities of the enemy in great contempt, and never would admit the possibility of defeat where the odds against him were not much over two to one.[155]

In popular culture

The bluegrass band The Dixie Bee-Liners have a biographical ballad about Jones on their 2008 album *Ripe* (Pinecastle Records) entitled "Grumble Jones". The song was co-written by band members Buddy Woodward, Brandi Hart, and Blue Highway guitarist Tim Stafford.

A street in Centreville, Virginia is named Grumble Jones Court.[156]

References

- Eicher, John H., and David J. Eicher, *Civil War High Commands*. Stanford: Stanford University Press, 2001. ISBN 978-0-8047-3641-1.
- Lambert, Dobbie Edward. *Grumble: The W. E. Jones Brigade of 1863–64*. Wahiawa, HI: Lambert Enterprises, 1992.
- McClure, Alexander K., ed. *The Annals of the Civil War Written by Leading Participants North and South*. Philadelphia, PA: Times Publishing Company, 1879. ISBN 0963364103. ISBN 978-0963364104.
- Sifakis, Stewart. *Who Was Who in the Civil War*. New York: Facts On File, 1988. ISBN 978-0-8160-1055-4.
- Tagg, Larry. *The Generals of Gettysburg*[157]. Campbell, CA: Savas Publishing, 1998. ISBN 1-882810-30-9.
- Warner, Ezra J. *Generals in Gray: Lives of the Confederate Commanders*. Baton Rouge: Louisiana State University Press, 1959. ISBN 978-0-8071-0823-9.
- "The Dixie Bee-Liners"[158]
- 'maps.google.com Grumble Jones Ct. Centreville, VA 20121'[159] Retrieved February 2, 2012.

Further reading

- Patchan, Scott C. *The Battle of Piedmont and Hunter's Campaign for Staunton: The 1864 Shenandoah Campaign*. Charleston: The History Press, 2011. ISBN 978-1-60949-197-0.
- Wert, Jeffry D. *Cavalryman of the Lost Cause: A Biography of J.E.B. Stuart*. New York: Simon & Schuster, 2008. ISBN 978-0-7432-7819-5.

External links

- Online biography[160]
- "William E. Jones"[161]. Find a Grave. Retrieved 2008-07-07.

Hugh Judson Kilpatrick

Hugh Judson Kilpatrick	
Born	January 14, 1836 Wantage Township, near Deckertown, New Jersey (now Sussex Borough)
Died	December 4, 1881 (aged 45) Santiago, Chile
Place of burial	West Point Cemetery
Allegiance	United States of America Union
Service/-branch	United States Army Union Army
Years of service	1861–1865
Rank	★★★ Major General
Battles/wars	American Civil War

Hugh Judson Kilpatrick (January 14, 1836 – December 4, 1881) was an officer in the Union Army during the American Civil War, achieving the rank of brevet major general. He was later the United States Minister to Chile, and a failed political candidate for the U.S. House of Representatives.

Known as "Kilcavalry" (or "Kill-Cavalry") for using tactics in battle that were considered as a reckless disregard for lives of soldiers under his command, Kilpatrick was both praised for the victories he achieved, and despised by southerners whose homes and towns he devastated.

Early life

Hugh Judson Kilpatrick, more commonly referred to as Judson Kilpatrick, the fourth child of Colonel Simon Kilpatrick and Julia Wickham, was born on the family farm in Wantage Township, near Deckertown, New Jersey (now Sussex Borough).

Civil War

Kilpatrick graduated from the United States Military Academy in 1861, just after the start of the war, and was commissioned a second lieutenant in the 1st U.S. Artillery. Within three days he was a captain in the 5th New York Infantry ("Duryée's Zouaves").

Kilpatrick was the first United States Army officer to be wounded in the Civil War, struck in the thigh by canister fire while leading a company at the Battle of Big Bethel, June 10, 1861. By September 25 he was a lieutenant colonel, now in the 2nd New York Cavalry, which he helped to raise, and it was the mounted arm that brought him fame and infamy.

Assignments were initially quiet for Lt. Col. Kilpatrick, serving in staff jobs and in minor cavalry skirmishes. That changed in the Second Battle of Bull Run in August 1862. He raided the Virginia Central Railroad early in the campaign and then ordered a foolish twilight cavalry charge the first evening of the battle, losing a full squadron of troopers. Nevertheless, he was promoted to full colonel on December 6.

Kilpatrick was aggressive, fearless, ambitious, and blustery. He was a master, in his mid-twenties, of using political influence to get ahead. His men had little love for his manner and his willingness to exhaust men and horses and to order suicidal mounted cavalry charges. (The rifled muskets introduced to warfare in the 1850s made the historic cavalry charge essentially an anachronism. Cavalry's role shrank primarily to screening, raiding, and reconnaissance.) The widespread nickname they used for Kilpatrick was "Kill Cavalry". He also had a bad reputation with others in the Army. His camps were poorly maintained and frequented by prostitutes, often visiting Kilpatrick himself. He was jailed in 1862 on charges of corruption, accused of selling captured Confederate goods for personal gain. He was jailed again for a drunken spree in Washington, D.C., and for allegedly accepting bribes in the procurement of horses for his command.

In February 1863, Maj. Gen. Joseph Hooker created a Cavalry Corps in the Army of the Potomac, commanded by Maj. Gen. George Stoneman. Kilpatrick assumed command of the 1st Brigade, 2nd Division. In the Chancellorsville Campaign in May, Stoneman's cavalry was ordered to swing deeply

Figure 25: *Harper's Weekly rendering of Kilpatrick's raid*

behind Gen. Robert E. Lee's army and destroy railroads and supplies. Kilpatrick did just that, with gusto. Although the corps failed to distract Lee as intended, Kilpatrick achieved fame by aggressively capturing wagons, burning bridges, and riding around Lee, almost to the outskirts of Richmond, Virginia, in Stoneman's 1863 Raid.

Gettysburg Campaign

At the beginning of the Gettysburg Campaign, on June 9, 1863, Kilpatrick fought at Brandy Station, the largest cavalry battle of the war. He received his brigadier general's star on June 13, fought at Aldie and Upperville, and assumed division command three days before the Battle of Gettysburg commenced. On June 30, he clashed briefly with J.E.B. Stuart's cavalry at Hanover, Pennsylvania, but then proceeded on a wild goose chase in pursuit of Stuart, rather than fulfilling his mission of intelligence gathering.

On the second day of the Gettysburg battle, July 2, 1863, Kilpatrick's division skirmished against Wade Hampton five miles northeast of town at Hunterstown. He then settled in for the night to the southeast at Two Taverns. One of his famous brigade commanders, Brig. Gen. George A. Custer, was ordered to join Brig. Gen. David McM. Gregg's division for the next day's action against Stuart's cavalry east of town, so Kilpatrick was down to one brigade. On July 3, after Pickett's Charge, he was ordered by army commander Maj.

Figure 26: *Union Cavalry General Hugh Judson Kilpatrick*

Gen. George G. Meade and Cavalry Corps commander Alfred Pleasonton to launch a cavalry charge against the infantry positions of Lt. Gen. James Longstreet's Corps on the Confederate right flank, just west of Little Round Top. Kilpatrick's lone brigade commander, Brig. Gen. Elon J. Farnsworth, protested against the futility of such a move. Kilpatrick essentially questioned his bravery and allegedly dared him to charge: "Then, by God, if you are afraid to go I will lead the charge myself." Farnsworth reluctantly complied with the order. He was killed in the attack and his brigade suffered significant losses.

Kilpatrick and the rest of the cavalry pursued and harassed Lee during his retreat back to Virginia. That fall, he took part in an expedition to destroy the Confederate gunboats *Satellite* and *Reliance* in the Rappahannock River, boarding them and capturing their crews successfully.

The Dahlgren Affair

Just before the start of Lt. Gen. Ulysses S. Grant's Overland Campaign in the spring of 1864, Kilpatrick conducted a raid toward Richmond and through the Virginia Peninsula, hoping to rescue Union prisoners of war held at Belle Isle and in Libby Prisons in Richmond. Kilpatrick took his division out on February 28, sneaking past Robert E. Lee's flank and driving south for Richmond. On March 1, they were within 5 miles of the city. Defenses around

Figure 27: *Kilpatrick and his 3rd Division staff, March 1864*

the city were too strong however and numerous squads of Confederate militia
and cavalry nipped at their heels the whole way, including some of General
Wade Hampton's troopers dispatched from the Army of Northern Virginia.
Unable to get at Richmond or return to the Army of the Potomac, Kilpatrick
decided to bolt down the Virginia Peninsula where Ben Butler's Army of the
James was stationed. Meanwhile, the general was dismayed to find out that Ul-
ric Dahlgren's brigade (detached from the main force) had not made it across
the James River. Eventually 300 of the latter's troopers stumbled into camp,
Dahlgren and the rest seemingly vanished into thin air. The survivors reported
that they'd made a nightmarish journey through the countryside around Richmond in darkness and a sleet storm, the woods filled with enemy troops and
hostile civilians at every turn. Dahlgren and the 200 cavalrymen he was ac-
companying had been told by a slave of a place where the James was shallow
and could be forded. When they got there, the river was swelled up and crest-
ing. Convinced he'd been tricked, Dahlgren ordered the slave hanged. They
went back north and found that Kilpatrick was gone and they were alone in a
hostile country. The troopers battled their way to the Mattaponi River, crossed,
and appeared to be safe from danger, but in the dark they ran into a Confederate ambush. Dahlghren was shot dead along with many of his men, the rest being taken prisoner. His body was then displayed in Richmond as a war trophy.
Papers found on the body of Dahlgren shortly after his death which described

the object of the expedition, and they were apparently altered to read that he wanted to burn and loot Richmond and assassinate Jefferson Davis and the whole Confederate cabinet.

The raid had resulted in 324 cavalrymen killed and wounded, and 1000 more taken prisoner. In addition, Kilpatrick's men had cut a swathe of destruction across the outskirts of Richmond, destroying tobacco barns, boats, railroad cars and tracks, and other infrastructure. They also deposited a large number of pamphlets in and around homes and other buildings offering amnesty to any Southern civilian who took the oath of loyalty to the United States.

The discovery and publication of the Dahlgren Papers sparked an international controversy. General Braxton Bragg denounced the papers as "fiendish" and Confederate Secretary of War James Seddon proposed that the Union prisoners be hanged. Robert E. Lee agreed that they made for an atrocious document, but urged calm, saying that no actual destruction had taken place and the papers might very well be fakes. In addition, Lee was concerned because some Confederate guerrillas had just been captured by the Army of the Potomac, which was considering hanging them, and execution of Dalghren's men might set off a chain reaction. The Confederate general sent the papers to George Meade under a flag of truce and asked him to provide an explanation. Meade wrote back that no burnings or assassinations had been ordered by anyone in Washington or the army. Meanwhile, newspapers and politicians in the North and South exchanged blows. The former condemned the use of Ulrich Dahlgren's corpse as a carnival attraction and the latter accused Lincoln's government of wanting to conduct indiscriminate pillage and slaughter on Virginia civilians, including the claim that Kilpatrick wanted to free Union prisoners and turn them loose on the women of Richmond. Northern papers also cheered the destruction caused by the raid and took pleasure in describing the ravaged condition of the Virginia countryside. After reaching Ben Butler's base at Fort Monroe, Kilpatrick's men took a steamship back to Washington. More trouble followed when they were granted a few days' rest in Alexandria, Virginia before rejoining the Army of the Potomac. The city was garrisoned with African-American troops, and one stopped to inform a cavalryman that only persons on active duty were allowed to ride horses through the streets. This trooper found it insulting to take orders from a black man and promptly struck him down with his sword. Kilpatrick's division was punished by being forced to immediately embark for the Rapidan River without resting or drawing new uniforms.

The "Kilpatrick-Dahlgren" expedition was such a fiasco that Kilpatrick found he was no longer welcome in the Eastern Theater. He transferred west to command the 3rd Division of the Cavalry Corps of the Army of the Cumberland, under Maj. Gen. William Tecumseh Sherman.

Final campaigns through Georgia and the Carolinas

Summing up Judson Kilpatrick in 1864, Sherman said "I know that Kilpatrick is a hell of a damned fool, but I want just that sort of man to command my cavalry on this expedition."

Starting in May 1864, Kilpatrick rode in the Atlanta Campaign. On May 13, he was severely wounded in the thigh at the Battle of Resaca and his injuries kept him out of the field until late July. He had considerable success raiding behind Confederate lines, tearing up railroads, and at one point rode his division completely around the enemy positions in Atlanta. His division played a significant role in the Battle of Jonesborough on August 31, 1864.

Kilpatrick continued with Sherman through his March to the Sea to Savannah and north in the Carolinas Campaign. He delighted in destroying Southern property. On two occasions his coarse personal instincts betrayed him: Confederate cavalry under the command of Maj. Gen. Wade Hampton raided his camp while he was in bed with a young Southern woman he had met while going through Columbia, and, at the Battle of Monroe's Crossroads, he was forced to flee for his life in his underclothes until his troops could reform. Kilpatrick accompanied Maj. Gen. William T. Sherman to the surrender negotiations held at Bennett Place near Durham, North Carolina, on April 17, 1865.

Kilpatrick later commanded a division of the Cavalry Corps in the Military Division of the Mississippi from April to June 1865, and was promoted to major general of volunteers on June 18, 1865.

Later life

Kilpatrick became active in politics as a Republican and in 1880 was an unsuccessful candidate for the U.S. Congress from New Jersey.

In 1865, Kilpatrick was appointed Minister to Chile by President Andrew Johnson, and he was continued in that office by President Grant. As American Minister to Chile, he was involved in an attempt to arbitrate between the combatants of the Chincha Islands War after the Valparaiso bombardment (1866). The attempt failed, as the chief condition of Spanish admiral Méndez Núñez was the return of the captured *Covadonga*. Kilpatrick asked the American naval commander Commander John Rodgers to defend the port and attack the Spanish fleet. Admiral Méndez Núñez famously responded with, "I will be forced to sink [the US ships], because even if I have one ship left I will proceed with the bombardment. Spain, the Queen and I prefer honor without ships to ships without honor." (*"España prefiere honra sin barcos a barcos sin honra."*)

Kilpatrick was recalled in 1870. The 1865 appointment seems to have been the result of a political deal. Kilpatrick had been a candidate for the Republican nomination for governor of New Jersey but lost out to Marcus Ward. Due to his service in helping Ward, Kilpatrick was rewarded with the post in Chile. Due to the Grant administration recalling him, Kilpatrick supported Horace Greeley in the 1872 presidential election. By 1876, Kilpatrick returned to the Republicans and supported Rutherford B. Hayes for the presidency.

In Chile he married, as his second wife, Luisa Fernandez de Valdivieso, {1836-1928}[162] a member of a wealthy family of Spanish origin that had emigrated to South America in the 17th century. They had two daughters: Julia Mercedes Kilpatrick {b.Nov 6, 1867 Santiago, Chile -d ? Married Nov 7, 1894 to William Carroll Rafferty} and Laura Delphine Kilpatrick {1874-1956} married June 29, 1897[163] to Harry Hays Morgan {b.1859 New Orleans-d.England 1933; son of Philip H. Morgan} {divorced 1927}. Laura Kilpatrick and Harry Morgan were the parents of twins sisters Thelma, Viscountess Furness and Gloria Morgan Vanderbilt; Artist and socialite Gloria Vanderbilt (born 1924) is Hugh Judson Kilpatrick's great-granddaughter. Another prominent descendant is CNN newsman Anderson Cooper, Kilpatrick's great-great-grandson.

In March 1881, in recognition of Kilpatrick's service to the Republicans in New Jersey as well as a consolation prize for his defeat for a House seat, President James Garfield appointed Kilpatrick again to the post of Minister to Chile, where he died shortly after his arrival in the Chilean capital Santiago. His remains returned to the United States in 1887 and were interred at the West Point Cemetery in West Point, New York.

Kilpatrick was the author of two plays, *Allatoona: An Historical and Military Drama in Five Acts* (1875) and *The Blue and the Gray: Or, War is Hell* (posthumous, 1930).

Legacy

Battery Kilpatrick at Fort Sherman, on the Atlantic end of the Panama Canal, was named for Judson Kilpatrick.[164,165]

References

- Eicher, John H.; David J. Eicher (2001). *'Civil War High Commands*. Stanford, Calif.: Stanford University Press. ISBN 0-8047-3641-3. OCLC 45917117[166].
- Johnson, Robert Underwood; Clarence C. Buel (eds.) (1884–1888). *Battles and Leaders of the Civil War*[167]. New York: Century Co. ISBN 1-4179-4500-1. OCLC 2048818[168].

- Lewis, Lloyd (1958) [1932]. *Sherman: Fighting Prophet.* Harcourt, Brace. OCLC 497732[169].
- Martin, Samuel J. (2000). *Kill-Cavalry: The Life of Union General Hugh Judson Kilpatrick.* Mechanicsburg, Pa.: Stackpole Books. ISBN 0-8117-0887-X. OCLC 42428710[170].
- Pierce, John Edward (1983). "General Hugh Judson Kilpatrick in the American Civil War". Thesis (Ph. D.)–Pennsylvania State University. OCLC 11893938[171].
- Schultz, Duane (1999). *The Dahlgren Affair: Terror and Conspiracy in the Civil War.* New York: W. W. Norton. ISBN 0-393-31986-5. OCLC 53405397[172].
- Snell, James P.; W. W. Clayton (1881). *History of Sussex and Warren Counties, New Jersey.* Philadelphia: Everts & Peck. OCLC 14075041[173].
- Spera, W. H. (1911). "Kilpatrick's Richmond Raid". In H. P. Moyer. *History of the Seventeenth Regiment Pennsylvania Volunteer Cavalry.* Lebanon, Pa.: Sowers Printing Company. OCLC 1881547[174].
- Tagg, Larry (1998). *The Generals of Gettysburg: The Leaders of America's Greatest Battle*[175]. 1-882810-30-9: Savas Pub. Co. ISBN 0-306-81242-8. OCLC 39725526[176].

External links

- Gettysburg Discussion Group research article[177]

Diplomatic posts		
Preceded by **Thomas H. Nelson**	**United States Envoy to Chile** March 12, 1866 – August 3, 1870	Succeeded by **Joseph Pomeroy Root**
Preceded by **Thomas A. Osborn**	**United States Envoy to Chile** July 25, 1881 – December 2, 1881	Succeeded by **Cornelius A. Logan**

John Sedgwick

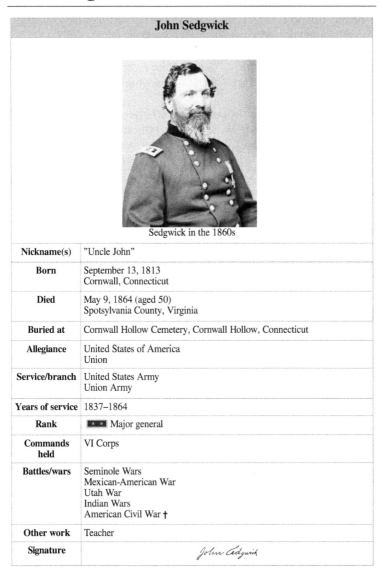

	John Sedgwick
	Sedgwick in the 1860s
Nickname(s)	"Uncle John"
Born	September 13, 1813 Cornwall, Connecticut
Died	May 9, 1864 (aged 50) Spotsylvania County, Virginia
Buried at	Cornwall Hollow Cemetery, Cornwall Hollow, Connecticut
Allegiance	United States of America Union
Service/branch	United States Army Union Army
Years of service	1837–1864
Rank	Major general
Commands held	VI Corps
Battles/wars	Seminole Wars Mexican-American War Utah War Indian Wars American Civil War †
Other work	Teacher
Signature	*John Sedgwick*

John Sedgwick (September 13, 1813 – May 9, 1864) was a teacher, a career military officer, and a Union Army general in the American Civil War. He was wounded three times at the Battle of Antietam while leading his division in an unsuccessful assault, causing him to miss the Battle of Fredericksburg. Under his command, the VI Corps played an important role in the Chancellorsville

Campaign by engaging Confederate troops at the Second Battle of Fredericksburg and the Battle of Salem Church. His Corps was the last to arrive at the Battle of Gettysburg, and thus did not see much action. Sedgwick was killed by a sharpshooter at the Battle of Spotsylvania Court House on May 9, 1864, making him the highest ranking United States soldier to be killed in the war. He is well-remembered for his ironic last words: "They couldn't hit an elephant at this distance."

Early life and education

Sedgwick was born in the Litchfield Hills town of Cornwall, Connecticut. He was named after his grandfather, John Sedgwick (brother of Theodore Sedgwick), an American Revolutionary War general who served with George Washington. He attended Sharon Academy for 2 years and Cheshire Academy in 1830-31, After teaching for two years, he attended the United States Military Academy, graduated in 1837 ranked 24th of 50, and was commissioned a second lieutenant in the U.S. Army's artillery branch. He fought in the Seminole Wars and received two brevet promotions in the Mexican-American War, to captain for Contreras and Churubusco, and to major for Chapultepec. After returning from Mexico he transferred to the cavalry and served in Kansas, in the Utah War, and in the Indian Wars, participating in 1857 in a punitive expedition against the Cheyenne.[178]

In the summer and fall of 1860, Sedgwick commanded an expedition to establish a new fort on the Platte River in what is now Colorado. This was a remote location with no railroads, and all supplies having to be carried long distances by riverboat, wagon train or horseback.[179] Even though many of these supplies failed to arrive, Sedgwick still managed to erect comfortable stone buildings for his men before the cold weather set in.

American Civil War

At the start of the American Civil War, Sedgwick was serving as a colonel and Assistant Inspector General of the Military Department of Washington. He missed the early action of the war at the First Battle of Bull Run, recovering from cholera. Promoted to brigadier general on August 31, 1861, he commanded the 2nd brigade of Maj. Gen. Samuel P. Heintzelman's division in the Army of the Potomac, then his own division, which was designated the 2nd division of the II Corps for the Peninsula Campaign. In Virginia, he fought at Yorktown and Seven Pines and was wounded in the arm and leg at the Battle of Glendale. He was promoted to major general on July 4, 1862.

Figure 28: *Sedgwick during the Civil War.*

Figure 29: *General Sedgwick (seated right) with Colonels Albert V. Colburn and Delos B. Sackett in Harrison's Landing, Virginia, during the Peninsula Campaign in 1862.*

Figure 30: *Horse artillery headquarters in Brandy Station, Virginia, February 1864. Sedgwick stands at the far right between Generals George G. Meade and Alfred Torbert, along with staff officers.*

In the Battle of Antietam, II Corps commander Maj. Gen. Edwin V. Sumner impulsively sent Sedgwick's division in a mass assault without proper reconnaissance. His division was engaged by Confederate forces under Maj. Gen. Thomas J. "Stonewall" Jackson from three sides, was routed, and fell back with barely half the men it had started with. Sedgwick himself was hit by three bullets, in the wrist, leg, and shoulder, and was out of action until after the Battle of Fredericksburg.

From December 26, 1862, he briefly led the II Corps and the IX Corps, and then finally the VI Corps of the Army of the Potomac, which he commanded until his death in 1864. During the Battle of Chancellorsville, his corps faced Fredericksburg in an initial holding action while Maj. Gen. Joseph Hooker's other four corps maneuvered against Robert E. Lee's left flank. He was slow to take action, but eventually crossed the Rappahannock River and assaulted Maj. Gen. Jubal Early's small force on Marye's Heights on May 3 during the Second Battle of Fredericksburg. Moving west slowly to join forces with Hooker and trap Lee between the halves of the army, he was stopped by elements of Lee's Second Corps (under Maj. Gen. J.E.B. Stuart, following the wounding of Jackson) at the Battle of Salem Church, forcing his eventual retreat back over the Rappahannock.

At the Battle of Gettysburg, his corps arrived late on July 2 and as a result only a few units were able to take part in the final Union counterattacks in the Wheatfield. It was not kept together as a unit during the second and third days of the battle, its brigades scattered around to plug holes in the line. While much of Sedgwick's VI Corps was held in reserve at Gettysburg, it performed exceptionally at the battle of Rappahannock Station in November, capturing four field pieces, eight stands of enemy colors and 1,700 prisoners.[180]

In the 1864 Overland Campaign, the VI Corps was on the Union right at the Battle of the Wilderness and defended against assaults by Lt. Gen. Richard S. Ewell's Second Corps.

Death

Sedgwick fell at the beginning of the Battle of Spotsylvania Court House, on May 9, 1864. His corps was probing skirmish lines ahead of the left flank of Confederate defenses and he was directing artillery placements. Confederate sharpshooters were about 1,000 yards (900 m) away and their shots caused members of his staff and artillerymen to duck for cover. Sedgwick strode around in the open and was quoted as saying, "What? Men dodging this way for single bullets? What will you do when they open fire along the whole line?" Although ashamed, his men continued to flinch and he said, "Why are you dodging like this? They couldn't hit an elephant at this distance."[181] Reports that he never finished the sentence are apocryphal, although the line was among his last words. He was shot moments later under the left eye and fell down dead.[182]

Sedgwick was the highest ranking Union death in the Civil War. Although Major General James B. McPherson was in command of an army at the time of his death and Sedgwick of a corps, Sedgwick had the most senior rank by date of all major generals killed. Upon hearing of his death, Lt. Gen. Ulysses S. Grant, flabbergasted by the news, repeatedly asked, "Is he really dead?"[183]

Legacy

Sedgwick's reputation was that of a solid, dependable, but relatively unaggressive general. He was well liked by his soldiers, who referred to him affectionately as "Uncle John". His death was met by universal sorrow; even Robert E. Lee expressed his sadness over the fate of an old friend. George G. Meade wept at the news. Ulysses S. Grant characterized Sedgwick as one who "was never at fault when serious work was to be done" and he told his staff that the loss for him was worse than that of an entire division.

John Sedgwick is buried near his birthplace of Cornwall Hollow, Connecticut. An equestrian statue honors him and the VI Corps at Gettysburg National Military Park.

There is a monument of General Sedgwick at West Point. Academy legend has it that a cadet who spins the rowels of the spurs on boots of the statue at

Figure 31: *Monument to commemorate the death of General John Sedgwick at Spotsylvania National Military Park, Virginia*

Figure 32: *A statue of General Sedgwick at West Point*

midnight while wearing full parade dress gray over white uniform under arms will have good luck on his or her final exam.

The following were named in his honor:

- Sedgwick, Arkansas
- Sedgwick, Colorado
- Sedgwick County, Colorado
- Sedgwick, Kansas
- Sedgwick County, Kansas
- Fort Sedgwick was one of the forts of the Union siege line in the Siege of Petersburg 1864-65[184]
- Camp Rankin was renamed Fort Sedgwick in 1865, near Julesburg, Colorado[185]

A major street in the Bronx, in New York City, is named after him. An east-west street in Washington, D.C. near American University is also named in his honor, as is another on Chicago's near north side. Grand Army of the Republic Post #4 in Keene, New Hampshire; Post #12 in Milwaukee, Wisconsin; Post #17 in Santa Ana, California; and Post #37 in York, Pennsylvania are all named after him. Also, a junior high-school (John Sedgwick Junior High "Home of the Generals") in Port Orchard, Washington, was named after him.

In the 1990 film *Dances with Wolves*, Lt. John Dunbar (Kevin Costner) stays at a fictional Fort Sedgwick, presumably named after General Sedgwick. The fort in the film may have been inspired by the Fort Sedgwick built in Colorado in 1860.

Farley, his headquarters at the time of the Battle of Brandy Station, was listed on the National Register of Historic Places in 1976.

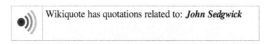

Wikiquote has quotations related to: *John Sedgwick*

Wikimedia Commons has media related to *John Sedgwick*.

Notes

Footnotes

Citations

References

- Berthrong, Donald J. *The Southern Cheyenne*. Norman: University of Oklahoma Press, 1979. OCLC 254915143[186]
- Eicher, John H., and David J. Eicher. *Civil War High Commands*. Stanford, CA: Stanford University Press, 2001. ISBN 0-8047-3641-3.
- Foote, Shelby. *The Civil War: A Narrative*. vol. 3, *Red River to Appomattox*. New York: Random House, 1974. ISBN 0-394-74913-8.
- Grinnell, George Bird. *The Fighting Cheyennes*. Norman: University of Oklahoma Press, 1956. OCLC 419857[187]. First published 1915 by Charles Scribner's Sons.
- Jurgen, Robert J., and Allan Keller. *Major General John Sedgwick, U.S. Volunteers, 1813-1864*. Hartford: Connecticut Civil War Centennial Committee, 1963.
- Rhea, Gordon C. *The Battles for Spotsylvania Court House and the Road to Yellow Tavern May 7–12, 1864*. Baton Rouge: Louisiana State University Press, 1997. ISBN 0-8071-2136-3.
- Sifakis, Stewart. *Who Was Who In The Civil War*. New York: Facts on File, 1988. ISBN 0-8160-1055-2.
- Winslow, Richard Elliott. *General John Sedgwick: The Story of a Union Corps Commander*. Novato, CA: Presidio Press, 1982. ISBN 0-89141-030-9.

External links

- Death of General John Sedgwick[188]
- Short biographical sketch[189]
- Another short bio[190]
- Tribute site[191]
- "John Sedgwick"[192]. Find a Grave. Retrieved 2008-11-01.

Preceded by Darius N. Couch	**Commander of the II Corps** December 26, 1862 – January 26, 1863	Succeeded by **Oliver O. Howard**
Preceded by **Orlando B. Wilcox**	**Commander of the IX Corps** January 16, 1863 - February 5, 1863	Succeeded by **William F. Smith**
Preceded by **John Newton** **James B. Ricketts**	**Commander of the VI Corps** February 5, 1863 - April 3, 1864 April 13, 1864 - May 9, 1864	Succeeded by **James B. Ricketts** **Horatio Wright**

J. E. B. Stuart

J. E. B. Stuart	

Birth name	James Ewell Brown Stuart
Nick-name(s)	"Jeb", "Beauty",[193] "Knight of the Golden Spurs",[194] "J.E.B."
Born	February 6, 1833 Patrick County, Virginia
Died	May 12, 1864 (aged 31) Richmond, Virginia
Buried at	Hollywood Cemetery
Allegiance	▨ United States of America ▨ Confederate States of America
Service/-branch	▨ United States Army ▨ Confederate States Army
Years of service	1854–1861 (USA) 1861–1864 (CSA)
Rank	▨ Captain (USA) ▨ Major general (CSA)
Commands held	Cavalry Corps, Army of Northern Virginia
Battles/-wars	Bleeding Kansas American Civil War • First Battle of Bull Run • Peninsula Campaign • Northern Virginia Campaign • Maryland Campaign • Battle of Fredericksburg • Battle of Chancellorsville • Gettysburg Campaign • Overland Campaign 　• Battle of Yellow Tavern †
Signature	*J.E.B.Stuart*

James Ewell Brown "Jeb" Stuart (February 6, 1833 – May 12, 1864) was a United States Army officer from the U.S. state of Virginia, who later became a Confederate States Army general during the American Civil War. He was known to his friends as "Jeb", from the initials of his given names. Stuart was a cavalry commander known for his mastery of reconnaissance and the use of cavalry in support of offensive operations. While he cultivated a cavalier image (red-lined gray cape, yellow sash, hat cocked to the side with an ostrich plume, red flower in his lapel, often sporting cologne), his serious work made him the trusted eyes and ears of Robert E. Lee's army and inspired Southern morale.[195]

Stuart graduated from West Point in 1854, and served in Texas and Kansas with the U.S. Army. He was a veteran of the frontier conflicts with Native Americans and the violence of Bleeding Kansas, and he participated in the capture of John Brown at Harpers Ferry.

He resigned when his home state of Virginia seceded to serve in the Confederate Army, first under Stonewall Jackson in the Shenandoah Valley, but then in increasingly important cavalry commands of the Army of Northern Virginia, playing a role in all of that army's campaigns until his death. He established a reputation as an audacious cavalry commander and on two occasions (during the Peninsula Campaign and the Maryland Campaign) circumnavigated the Union Army of the Potomac, bringing fame to himself and embarrassment to the North. At the Battle of Chancellorsville, he distinguished himself as a temporary commander of the wounded Stonewall Jackson's infantry corps.

Arguably Stuart's most famous campaign, Gettysburg, was marred when he was surprised by a Union cavalry attack at the Battle of Brandy Station and by his separation from Lee's army for an extended period, leaving Lee unaware of Union troop movements and contributing to the Confederate defeat at the Battle of Gettysburg. Stuart received significant criticism from the Southern press as well as the postbellum proponents of the Lost Cause movement, but historians have failed to agree on whether Stuart's exploit was entirely the fault of his judgment or simply a result of bad luck and Lee's less-than-explicit orders.

During the 1864 Overland Campaign, Union Maj. Gen. Philip Sheridan's cavalry launched an offensive to defeat Stuart, who was mortally wounded at the Battle of Yellow Tavern. Stuart's widow wore black for the rest of her life in remembrance of her deceased husband.

Figure 33: *A young Stuart*

Early life

Stuart was born at Laurel Hill Farm, a plantation in Patrick County, Virginia, near the border with North Carolina. He was of Scottish American and Scots-Irish background.[196] He was the eighth of eleven children and the youngest of the five sons to survive past early age.[197] His great-grandfather, Major Alexander Stuart, commanded a regiment at the Battle of Guilford Court House during the American Revolutionary War.[198] His father, Archibald Stuart, was a War of 1812 veteran, slaveholder, attorney, and Democratic politician who represented Patrick County in both houses of the Virginia General Assembly, and also served one term in the United States House of Representatives.[199] Archibald was a cousin of Alexander Hugh Holmes Stuart. Elizabeth Letcher Pannill Stuart, Jeb's mother, who was known as a strict religious woman with a good sense for business, ran the family farm.

Education

Stuart was educated at home by his mother and tutors until the age of twelve, when he left Laurel Hill to be educated by various teachers in Wytheville, Virginia, and at the home of his aunt Anne (Archibald's sister) and her husband Judge James Ewell Brown (Stuart's namesake) at Danville.[200] He entered

Emory and Henry College when he was fifteen, and attended from 1848 to 1850.[201]

During the summer of 1848, Stuart attempted to enlist in the U.S. Army, but was rejected as underaged. He obtained an appointment in 1850 to the United States Military Academy at West Point, New York, from Representative Thomas Hamlet Averett, the man who had defeated his father in the 1848 election.[202] Stuart was a popular student and was happy at the Academy. Although not handsome in his teen years, his classmates called him by the nickname "Beauty", which they described as his "personal comeliness in inverse ratio to the term employed."[203] He possessed a chin "so short and retiring as positively to disfigure his otherwise fine countenance." He quickly grew a beard after graduation and a fellow officer remarked that he was "the only man he ever saw that [a] beard improved."[204]

Robert E. Lee was appointed superintendent of the Academy in 1852, and Stuart became a friend of the Lee family, seeing them socially on frequent occasions. Lee's nephew, Fitzhugh Lee, also arrived at the academy in 1852. In Stuart's final year, in addition to achieving the cadet rank of second captain of the corps, he was one of eight cadets designated as honorary "cavalry officers" for his skills in horsemanship.[205] Stuart graduated 13th in his class of 46 in 1854. He ranked tenth in his class in cavalry tactics. Although he enjoyed the civil engineering curriculum at the academy and did well in mathematics, his poor drawing skills hampered his engineering studies, and he finished 29th in that discipline. A Stuart family tradition says he deliberately degraded his academic performance in his final year to avoid service in the elite, but dull, Corps of Engineers.[206]

United States Army

Stuart was commissioned a brevet second lieutenant and assigned to the U.S. Regiment of Mounted Riflemen in Texas. After an arduous journey, he reached Fort Davis on January 28, 1855, and was a leader for three months on scouting missions over the San Antonio to El Paso Road.[207] He was soon transferred to the newly formed 1st Cavalry Regiment (1855) at Fort Leavenworth, Kansas Territory, where he became regimental quartermaster[208] and commissary officer under the command of Col. Edwin V. Sumner.[209] He was promoted to first lieutenant in 1855.

Also in 1855, Stuart met Flora Cooke, the daughter of the commander of the 2nd U.S. Dragoon Regiment, Lieutenant Colonel Philip St. George Cooke. Burke Davis described Flora as "an accomplished horsewoman, and though not pretty, an effective charmer," to whom "Stuart succumbed with hardly a struggle."[210] They became engaged in September, less than two months after meeting. Stuart humorously wrote of his rapid courtship in Latin, *"Veni, Vidi, Victus sum"* (I came, I saw, I was conquered). Although a gala wedding was planned for Fort Riley, Kansas, the death of Stuart's father on September 20 caused a change of plans and the marriage on November 14 was small and limited to family witnesses.[211] The couple owned two slaves until 1859, one inherited from his father's estate, the other purchased.[212]

Stuart's leadership capabilities were soon recognized. He was a veteran of the frontier conflicts with Native Americans and the antebellum violence of Bleeding Kansas. He was wounded on July 29, 1857, while fighting at Solomon River, Kansas, against the Cheyenne. Col. Sumner ordered a charge with drawn sabers against a wave of Indian arrows. Scattering the warriors, Stuart and three other lieutenants chased one down, whom Stuart wounded in the thigh with his pistol. The Cheyenne turned and fired at Stuart with an old-fashioned pistol, striking him in the chest with a bullet, which did little more damage than to pierce the skin.[213] Stuart returned in September to Fort Leavenworth and was reunited with his wife.

Their first child, a girl, had been born in 1856 but died the same day. On November 14, 1857, Flora gave birth to another daughter, whom the parents named Flora after her mother. The family relocated in early 1858 to Fort Riley, where they remained for three years.[214]

In 1859, Stuart developed a new piece of cavalry equipment, for which he received patent number 25,684 on October 4—a saber hook, or an "improved method of attaching sabers to belts." The U.S. government paid Stuart $5,000 for a "right to use" license and Stuart contracted with Knorr, Nece and Co. of Philadelphia to manufacture his hook. While in Washington, D.C., to discuss government contracts, and in conjunction with his application for an appointment into the quartermaster department, Stuart heard about John Brown's raid on the U.S. Arsenal at Harpers Ferry. Stuart volunteered to be aide-de-camp to Col. Robert E. Lee and accompanied Lee with a company of U.S. Marines from the Washington Navy Yard and four companies of Maryland militia. While delivering Lee's written surrender ultimatum to the leader of the group, who had been calling himself Isaac Smith, Stuart recognized "Old Ossawatomie Brown" from his days in Kansas.[215]

Stuart was promoted to captain on April 22, 1861, but resigned from the U.S. Army on May 3, 1861, to join the Confederate States Army, following the secession of Virginia. (His letter of resignation, sent from Cairo, Illinois, was accepted by the War Department on May 14.)[216] Upon learning that his father-in-law, Col. Cooke, would remain in the U.S. Army during the coming war, Stuart wrote to his brother-in-law (future Confederate Brig. Gen. John Rogers Cooke), "He will regret it but once, and that will be continuously."[217] On June 26, 1860, Flora gave birth to a son, Philip St. George Cooke Stuart, but his father changed the name to James Ewell Brown Stuart, Jr. ("Jimmie"), in late 1861 out of disgust with his father-in-law.[218]

Confederate Army

Early service

Stuart was commissioned as a lieutenant colonel of Virginia Infantry in the Confederate Army on May 10, 1861. Maj. Gen. Robert E. Lee, now commanding the armed forces of Virginia, ordered him to report to Colonel Thomas J. Jackson at Harper's Ferry. Jackson chose to ignore Stuart's infantry designation and assigned him on July 4 to command all the cavalry companies of the Army of the Shenandoah, organized as the 1st Virginia Cavalry Regiment.[219] He was promoted to colonel on July 16.

General Joseph E. Johnston, letter to Confederate President Jefferson Davis, August 1861[220]

After early service in the Shenandoah Valley, Stuart led his regiment in the First Battle of Bull Run, and participated in the pursuit of the retreating Federals. He then commanded the Army's outposts along the upper Potomac River until given command of the cavalry brigade for the army then known as the Army of the Potomac (later named the Army of Northern Virginia). He was promoted to brigadier general on September 24, 1861.

Peninsula

In 1862, the Union Army of the Potomac began its Peninsula Campaign against Richmond, Virginia, and Stuart's cavalry brigade assisted Gen. Joseph E. Johnston's army as it withdrew up the Virginia Peninsula in the face of superior numbers. Stuart fought at the Battle of Williamsburg, but in general the terrain and weather on the Peninsula did not lend themselves to cavalry operations. However, when Gen. Robert E. Lee became commander of the Army of Northern Virginia, he requested that Stuart perform reconnaissance to determine whether the right flank of the Union army was vulnerable. Stuart set out with 1,200 troopers on the morning of June 12 and, having determined that the flank was indeed vulnerable, took his men on a complete circumnavigation of the Union army, returning after 150 miles on July 15 with 165 captured Union soldiers, 260 horses and mules, and various quartermaster and ordnance supplies. His men met no serious opposition from the more decentralized Union cavalry, coincidentally commanded by his father-in-law, Col. Cooke. The maneuver was a public relations sensation and Stuart was greeted with flower petals thrown in his path at Richmond. He had become as famous as Stonewall Jackson in the eyes of the Confederacy.[221]

Figure 34: *Confederate Cavalry General J.E.B. Stuart*

Northern Virginia

Early in the Northern Virginia Campaign, Stuart was promoted to major general on July 25, 1862, and his command was upgraded to the Cavalry Division.[222] He was nearly captured and lost his signature plumed hat and cloak to pursuing Federals during a raid in August, but in a retaliatory raid at Catlett's Station the following day, managed to overrun Union army commander Maj. Gen. John Pope's headquarters, and not only captured Pope's full uniform, but also intercepted orders that provided Lee with valuable intelligence concerning reinforcements for Pope's army.

At the Second Battle of Bull Run (Second Manassas), Stuart's cavalry followed the massive assault by Longstreet's infantry against Pope's army, protecting its flank with artillery batteries. Stuart ordered Brig. Gen. Beverly Robertson's brigade to pursue the Federals and in a sharp fight against Brig. Gen. John Buford's brigade, Col. Thomas T. Munford's 2nd Virginia Cavalry was overwhelmed until Stuart sent in two more regiments as reinforcements. Buford's men, many of whom were new to combat, retreated across Lewis's Ford and Stuart's troopers captured over 300 of them. Stuart's men harassed the retreating Union columns until the campaign ended at the Battle of Chantilly.[223]

Maryland

During the Maryland Campaign of September 1862, Stuart's cavalry screened the army's movement north. He bears some responsibility for Robert E. Lee's lack of knowledge of the position and celerity of the pursuing Army of the Potomac under George B. McClellan. For a five-day period, Stuart rested his men and entertained local civilians at a gala ball at Urbana, Maryland. His reports make no reference to intelligence gathering by his scouts or patrols.[224] As the Union Army drew near to Lee's divided army, Stuart's men skirmished at various points on the approach to Frederick and Stuart was not able to keep his brigades concentrated enough to resist the oncoming tide. He misjudged the Union routes of advance, ignorant of the Union force threatening Turner's Gap, and required assistance from the infantry of Maj. Gen. D.H. Hill to defend the South Mountain passes in the Battle of South Mountain.[225] His horse artillery bombarded the flank of the Union army as it opened its attack in the Battle of Antietam. By mid-afternoon, Stonewall Jackson ordered Stuart to command a turning movement with his cavalry against the Union right flank and rear, which if successful would be followed up by an infantry attack from the West Woods. Stuart began probing the Union lines with more artillery barrages, which were answered with "murderous" counterbattery fire and the cavalry movement intended by Jackson was never launched.[226]

James I. Robertson, Jr., *Stonewall Jackson*[227]

Three weeks after Lee's army had withdrawn back to Virginia, on October 10–12, 1862, Stuart performed another of his audacious circumnavigations of the Army of the Potomac, his Chambersburg Raid—126 miles in under 60 hours, from Darkesville, West Virginia to as far north as Mercersburg, Pennsylvania and Chambersburg and around to the east through Emmitsburg, Maryland and south through Hyattstown, Maryland and White's Ford to Leesburg, Virginia—once again embarrassing his Union opponents and seizing horses and supplies, but at the expense of exhausted men and animals, without gaining much military advantage. Jubal Early referred to it as "the greatest horse stealing expedition" that only "annoyed" the enemy.[228] Stuart gave his friend Jackson a fine, new officer's tunic, trimmed with gold lace, commissioned from a Richmond tailor, which he thought would give Jackson more of the appearance of a proper general (something to which Jackson was notoriously indifferent).[229]

McClellan pushed his army slowly south, urged by President Lincoln to pursue Lee, crossing the Potomac starting on October 26. As Lee began moving to counter this, Stuart screened Longstreet's Corps and skirmished numerous times in early November against Union cavalry and infantry around Mountville, Aldie, and Upperville. On November 6, Stuart received sad news by telegram that his daughter Flora had died just before her fifth birthday of typhoid fever on November 3.[230]

Fredericksburg and Chancellorsville

In the December 1862 Battle of Fredericksburg, Stuart and his cavalry—most notably his horse artillery under Major John Pelham—protected Stonewall Jackson's flank at Hamilton's Crossing. General Lee commended his cavalry, which "effectually guarded our right, annoying the enemy and embarrassing his movements by hanging on his flank, and attacking when the opportunity occurred." Stuart reported to Flora the next day that he had been shot through his fur collar but was unhurt.[231]

After Christmas, Lee ordered Stuart to conduct a raid north of the Rappahannock River to "penetrate the enemy's rear, ascertain if possible his position & movements, & inflict upon him such damage as circumstances will permit." With 1,800 troopers and a horse artillery battery assigned to the operation, Stuart's raid reached as far north as four miles south of Fairfax Court House, seizing 250 prisoners, horses, mules, and supplies. Tapping telegraph lines, his signalmen intercepted messages between Union commanders and Stuart sent a personal telegram to Union Quartermaster General Montgomery C. Meigs, "General Meigs will in the future please furnish better mules; those you have furnished recently are very inferior."[232]

On March 17, 1863, Stuart's cavalry clashed with a Union raiding party at Kelly's Ford. The minor victory was marred by the death of Major Pelham, which caused Stuart profound grief, as he thought of him as close as a younger brother. He wrote to a Confederate Congressman, "The noble, the chivalric, the gallant Pelham is no more. ... Let the tears of agony we have shed, and the gloom of mourning throughout my command bear witness." Flora was pregnant at the time and Stuart told her that if it were a boy, he wanted him to be named John Pelham Stuart. (Virginia Pelham Stuart was born October 9.)[233]

At the Battle of Chancellorsville, Stuart accompanied Stonewall Jackson on his famous flanking march of May 2, 1863, and started to pursue the retreating soldiers of the Union XI Corps when he received word that both Jackson and his senior division commander, Maj. Gen. A.P. Hill, had been wounded. Hill, bypassing the next most senior infantry general in the corps, Brig. Gen. Robert E. Rodes, sent a message ordering Stuart to take command of the Second Corps. Although the delays associated with this change of command effectively ended the flanking attack the night of May 2, Stuart performed credibly as an infantry corps commander the following day, launching a strong and well-coordinated attack against the Union right flank at Chancellorsville. When Union troops abandoned Hazel Grove, Stuart had the presence of mind to quickly occupy

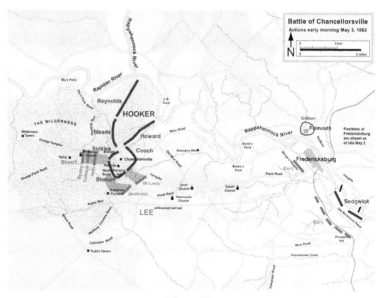

Figure 35:
Chancellorsville, May 3, 1863
Confederate/Rebels
Union/Federals/Army Of The Potomac

it and bombard the Union positions with artillery. Stuart relinquished his infantry command on May 6 when Hill returned to duty.[234] Stephen W. Sears wrote:

> ... It is hard to see how Jeb Stuart, in a new command, a cavalryman commanding infantry and artillery for the first time, could have done a better job. The astute Porter Alexander believed all credit was due: "Altogether, I do not think there was a more brilliant thing done in the war than Stuart's extricating that command from the extremely critical position in which he found it. "[235]

Stonewall Jackson died on May 10 and Stuart was once again devastated by the loss of a close friend, telling his staff that the death was a "national calamity." Jackson's wife, Mary Anna, wrote to Stuart on August 1, thanking him for a note of sympathy: "I need not assure you of which you already know, that your friendship & admiration were cordially reciprocated by him. I have frequently heard him speak of Gen'l Stuart as one of his warm personal friends, & also express admiration for your Soldierly qualities."[236]

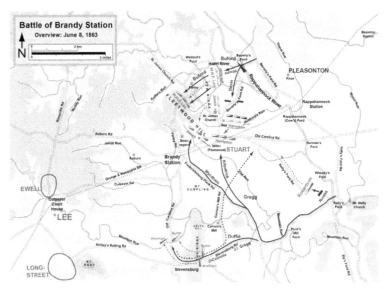

Figure 36: *Battle of Brandy Station, June 9, 1863*

Brandy Station

Stephen W. Sears, *Gettysburg*[237]

Returning to the cavalry for the Gettysburg Campaign, Stuart endured the two low points in his career, starting with the Battle of Brandy Station, the largest predominantly cavalry engagement of the war. By June 5, two of Lee's infantry corps were camped in and around Culpeper. Six miles northeast, holding the line of the Rappahannock River, Stuart bivouacked his cavalry troopers, mostly near Brandy Station, screening the Confederate Army against surprise by the enemy. Stuart requested a full field review of his troops by Gen. Lee. This grand review on June 5 included nearly 9,000 mounted troopers and four batteries of horse artillery, charging in simulated battle at Inlet Station, about two miles (three km) southwest of Brandy Station.[238]

Lee was not able to attend the review, however, so it was repeated in his presence on June 8, although the repeated performance was limited to a simple parade without battle simulations.[239] Despite the lower level of activity, some of the cavalrymen and the newspaper reporters at the scene complained that all Stuart was doing was feeding his ego and exhausting the horses. Lee ordered Stuart to cross the Rappahannock the next day and raid Union forward positions, screening the Confederate Army from observation or interference as it moved north. Anticipating this imminent offensive action, Stuart ordered his tired troopers back into bivouac around Brandy Station.[240]

Army of the Potomac commander Maj. Gen. Joseph Hooker interpreted Stuart's presence around Culpeper to be indicative of preparations for a raid on his army's supply lines. In reaction, he ordered his cavalry commander, Maj. Gen. Alfred Pleasonton, to take a combined arms force of 8,000 cavalrymen and 3,000 infantry on a "spoiling raid" to "disperse and destroy" the 9,500 Confederates.[241] Pleasonton's force crossed the Rappahannock in two columns on June 9, 1863, the first crossing at Beverly's Ford (Brig. Gen. John Buford's division) catching Stuart by surprise, waking him and his staff to the sound of gunfire. The second crossing, at Kelly's Ford, surprised Stuart again, and the Confederates found themselves assaulted from front and rear in a spirited melee of mounted combat. A series of confusing charges and countercharges swept back and forth across Fleetwood Hill, which had been Stuart's headquarters the previous night. After ten hours of fighting, Pleasonton ordered his men to withdraw across the Rappahannock.[242]

Richmond *Enquirer*, June 12, 1863[243]

Although Stuart claimed a victory because the Confederates held the field, Brandy Station is considered a tactical draw, and both sides came up short. Pleasonton was not able to disable Stuart's force at the start of an important campaign and he withdrew before finding the location of Lee's infantry nearby. However, the fact that the Southern cavalry had not detected the movement of two large columns of Union cavalry, and that they fell victim to a surprise attack, was an embarrassment that prompted serious criticism from fellow generals and the Southern press. The fight also revealed the increased competency of the Union cavalry, and foreshadowed the decline of the formerly invincible Southern mounted arm.[244]

Stuart's ride in the Gettysburg Campaign

Following a series of small cavalry battles in June as Lee's army began marching north through the Shenandoah Valley, Stuart may have had in mind the glory of circumnavigating the enemy army once again, desiring to erase the stain on his reputation of the surprise at Brandy Station. General Lee gave orders to Stuart on June 22 on how he was to participate in the march north, and the exact nature of those orders has been argued by the participants and historians ever since, but the essence was that he was instructed to guard the mountain passes with part of his force while the Army of Northern Virginia was still south of the Potomac and that he was to cross the river with the remainder of the army and screen the right flank of Ewell's Second Corps. Instead of taking a direct route north near the Blue Ridge Mountains, however, Stuart chose to reach Ewell's flank by taking his three best brigades (those of Brig. Gen. Wade Hampton, Brig. Gen. Fitzhugh Lee, and Col. John R. Chambliss, the latter replacing the wounded Brig. Gen. W.H.F. "Rooney" Lee) between the Union

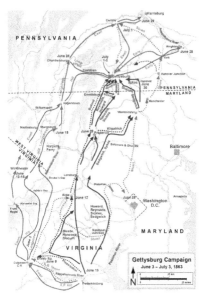

Figure 37: *Stuart's ride (shown with a red dotted line) during the Gettysburg Campaign, June 3 – July 3, 1863.*

army and Washington, moving north through Rockville to Westminster and on into Pennsylvania, hoping to capture supplies along the way and cause havoc near the enemy capital. Stuart and his three brigades departed Salem Depot at 1 a.m. on June 25.[245]

Unfortunately for Stuart's plan, the Union army's movement was underway and his proposed route was blocked by columns of Federal infantry, forcing him to veer farther to the east than either he or General Lee had anticipated. This prevented Stuart from linking up with Ewell as ordered and deprived Lee of the use of his prime cavalry force, the "eyes and ears" of the army, while advancing into unfamiliar enemy territory.[246]

Stuart's command crossed the Potomac River at 3 a.m. on June 28. At Rockville they captured a wagon train of 140 brand-new, fully loaded wagons and mule teams. This wagon train would prove to be a logistical hindrance to Stuart's advance, but he interpreted Lee's orders as placing importance on gathering supplies. The proximity of the Confederate raiders provoked some consternation in the national capital and two Union cavalry brigades and an artillery battery were sent to pursue the Confederates. Stuart supposedly said that were it not for his fatigued horses "he would have marched down the 7th Street Road [and] took Abe & Cabinet prisoners."[247]

In Westminster on June 29, his men clashed briefly with and overwhelmed two companies of Union cavalry, chasing them a long distance on the Baltimore road, which Stuart claimed caused a "great panic" in the city of Baltimore.[248] The head of Stuart's column encountered Brig. Gen. Judson Kilpatrick's cavalry as it passed through Hanover and scattered it on June 30; the Battle of Hanover ended after Kilpatrick's men regrouped and drove the Confederates out of town. Stuart's brigades had been better positioned to guard their captured wagon train than to take advantage of the encounter with Kilpatrick. After a 20-mile trek in the dark, his exhausted men reached Dover on the morning of July 1, as the Battle of Gettysburg was commencing without them.[249]

Stuart headed next for Carlisle, hoping to find Ewell. He lobbed a few shells into town during the early evening of July 1 and burned the Carlisle Barracks before withdrawing to the south towards Gettysburg. He and the bulk of his command reached Lee at Gettysburg the afternoon of July 2. He ordered Wade Hampton to cover the left rear of the Confederate battle lines, and Hampton fought with Brig. Gen. George Armstrong Custer at the Battle of Hunterstown before joining Stuart at Gettysburg.[250]

Gettysburg and its aftermath

When Stuart arrived at Gettysburg on the afternoon of July 2—bringing with him the caravan of captured Union supply wagons—he received a rare rebuke from Lee. (No one witnessed the private meeting between Lee and Stuart, but reports circulated at headquarters that Lee's greeting was "abrupt and frosty." Colonel Edward Porter Alexander wrote, "Although Lee said only, 'Well, General, you are here at last,' his manner implied rebuke, and it was so understood by Stuart."[251]) On the final day of the battle, Stuart was ordered to get into the enemy's rear and disrupt its line of communications at the same time Pickett's Charge was sent against the Union positions on Cemetery Ridge, but his attack on East Cavalry Field was repulsed by Union cavalry under Brig. Gens. David Gregg and George Custer.[252]

During the retreat from Gettysburg, Stuart devoted his full attention to supporting the army's movement, successfully screening against aggressive Union cavalry pursuit and escorting thousands of wagons with wounded men and captured supplies over difficult roads and through inclement weather. Numerous skirmishes and minor battles occurred during the screening and delaying actions of the retreat. Stuart's men were the final units to cross the Potomac River, returning to Virginia in "wretched condition—completely worn out and broken down."[253]

Confederate Maj. Gen. Henry Heth[254]

The Gettysburg Campaign was the most controversial of Stuart's career. He became one of the scapegoats (along with James Longstreet) blamed for Lee's loss at Gettysburg by proponents of the postbellum Lost Cause movement, such as Jubal Early.[255] This was fueled in part by opinions of less partisan writers, such as Stuart's subordinate, Thomas L. Rosser, who stated after the war that Stuart did, "on this campaign, *undoubtedly*, make the fatal blunder which lost us the battle of Gettysburg." In General Lee's report on the campaign, he wrote

> ... *the absence of the cavalry rendered it impossible to obtain accurate information. ... By the route [Stuart] pursued, the Federal Army was interposed between his command and our main body, preventing any communication with him until his arrival at Carlisle. The march toward Gettysburg was conducted more slowly than it would have been had the movements of the Federal Army been known.*

One of the most forceful postbellum defenses of Stuart was by Col. John S. Mosby, who had served under him during the campaign and was fiercely loyal to the late general, writing, "He made me all that I was in the war. ... But for his friendship I would never have been heard of." He wrote numerous articles for popular publications and published a book length treatise in 1908, a work that relied on his skills as a lawyer to refute categorically all of the claims laid against Stuart.[256]

Modern scholarship remains divided on Stuart's culpability. Edward G. Longacre argues that Lee deliberately gave Stuart wide discretion in his orders and had no complaints about Stuart's tardy arrival at Gettysburg because he established no date by which the cavalry was required to link up with Ewell. The 3½ brigades of cavalry left with the main army were adequate for Lee to negotiate enemy territory safely and that his choice not to use these brigades effectively cannot be blamed on Stuart. Edwin B. Coddington refers to the "tragedy" of Stuart in the Gettysburg Campaign and judges that when Fitzhugh Lee raised the question of "whether Stuart exercised the discretion *undoubtedly given to him, judiciously*," the answer is no. Nevertheless, replying to historians who maintain that Stuart's absence permitted Lee to be surprised at Gettysburg, Coddington points out that the Union commander, Maj. Gen. George Meade, was just as surprised, and the initial advantage lay with Lee. Eric J. Wittenberg and J. David Petruzzi have concluded that there was "plenty of blame to go around" and the fault should be divided between Stuart, the lack of specificity in Lee's orders, and Richard S. Ewell, who might have tried harder to link up with Stuart northeast of Gettysburg. Jeffry D. Wert acknowledges that Lee, his officers, and fighting by the Army of the Potomac bear the responsibility for the Confederate loss at Gettysburg, but states that "Stuart failed Lee and the army in the reckoning at Gettysburg. ... Lee trusted him and gave him discretion, but Stuart acted injudiciously."[257]

Although Stuart was not reprimanded or disciplined in any official way for his role in the Gettysburg campaign, it is noteworthy that his appointment to

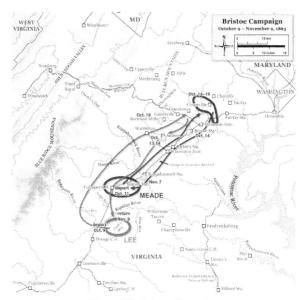

Figure 38: *Bristoe Campaign*

corps command on September 9, 1863, did not carry with it a promotion to lieutenant general. Edward Bonekemper wrote that since all other corps commanders in the Army of Northern Virginia carried this rank, Lee's decision to keep Stuart at major general rank, while at the same time promoting Stuart's subordinates Wade Hampton and Fitzhugh Lee to major generals, could be considered an implied rebuke.[258] Jeffry D. Wert wrote that there is no evidence Lee considered Stuart's performance during the Gettysburg Campaign and that it is "more likely that Lee thought the responsibilities in command of a cavalry corps did not equal those of an infantry corps."[259]

Fall 1863 and the 1864 Overland Campaign

Confederate Colonel Oliver Funsten[260]

Lee reorganized his cavalry on September 9, creating a Cavalry Corps for Stuart with two divisions of three brigades each. In the Bristoe Campaign, Stuart was assigned to lead a broad turning movement in an attempt to get into the enemy's rear, but General Meade skillfully withdrew his army without leaving Stuart any opportunities to take advantage of. On October 13, Stuart blundered into the rear guard of the Union III Corps near Warrenton. Ewell's corps was sent to rescue him, but Stuart hid his troopers in a wooded ravine until the unsuspecting III Corps moved on, and the assistance was not

Figure 39: *The 1864 Overland Campaign, including the Battle of Yellow Tavern*

necessary. As Meade withdrew towards Manassas Junction, brigades from the Union II Corps fought a rearguard action against Stuart's cavalry and the infantry of Brig. Gen. Harry Hays's division near Auburn on October 14. Stuart's cavalry boldly bluffed Warren's infantry and escaped disaster. After the Confederate repulse at Bristoe Station and an aborted advance on Centreville, Stuart's cavalry shielded the withdrawal of Lee's army from the vicinity of Manassas Junction. Judson Kilpatrick's Union cavalry pursued Stuart's cavalry along the Warrenton Turnpike, but were lured into an ambush near Chestnut Hill and routed. The Federal troopers were scattered and chased five miles (eight km) in an affair that came to be known as the "Buckland Races". The Southern press began to mute its criticism of Stuart's following his successful performance during the fall campaign.[261]

The Overland Campaign, Lt. Gen. Ulysses S. Grant's offensive against Lee in the spring of 1864, began at the Battle of the Wilderness, where Stuart aggressively pushed Thomas L. Rosser's Laurel Brigade into a fight against George Custer's better-armed Michigan Brigade, resulting in significant losses. General Lee sent a message to Stuart: "It is very important to save your Cavalry & not wear it out. ... You must use your good judgment to make any attack which may offer advantages." As the armies maneuvered toward their next confrontation at Spotsylvania Court House, Stuart's cavalry fought delaying actions against the Union cavalry. His defense at Laurel Hill, also directing the infantry of Brig. Gen. Joseph B. Kershaw, skillfully delayed the advance of the Federal army for nearly 5 critical hours.[262]

Yellow Tavern and death

The commander of the Army of the Potomac, Maj. Gen. George Meade, and his cavalry commander, Maj. Gen. Philip Sheridan, quarreled about the Union cavalry's performance in the first two engagements of the Overland Campaign. Sheridan heatedly asserted that he wanted to "concentrate all of cavalry, move out in force against Stuart's command, and whip it." Meade reported the comments to Grant, who replied "Did Sheridan say that? Well, he generally knows what he is talking about. Let him start right out and do it." Sheridan immediately organized a raid against Confederate supply and railroad lines close to Richmond, which he knew would bring Stuart to battle.[263]

Sheridan moved aggressively to the southeast, crossing the North Anna River and seizing Beaver Dam Station on the Virginia Central Railroad, where his men liberated a train carrying 3,000 Union prisoners and destroyed more than one million rations and medical supplies destined for Lee's army. Stuart dispatched a force of about 3,000 cavalrymen to intercept Sheridan's cavalry, which was more than three times their numbers. As he rode in pursuit, accompanied by his aide, Maj. Andrew R. Venable, they were able to stop briefly along the way to be greeted by Stuart's wife, Flora, and his children, Jimmie and Virginia. Venable wrote of Stuart, "He told me he never expected to live through the war, and that if we were conquered, that he did not want to live."[264]

The Battle of Yellow Tavern occurred May 11, at an abandoned inn located six miles (10 km) north of Richmond. The Confederate troopers tenaciously resisted from the low ridgeline bordering the road to Richmond, fighting for over three hours. A countercharge by the 1st Virginia Cavalry pushed the advancing Union troopers back from the hilltop as Stuart, on horseback, shouted encouragement while firing his revolver at the Union troopers. As the 5th Michigan Cavalry streamed in retreat past Stuart, a dismounted Union private, 44-year-old John A. Huff, turned and shot Stuart with his .44-caliber revolver from a distance of 10–30 yards.[265]

Huff's bullet struck Stuart in the left side. It then sliced through his stomach and exited his back, one inch to the right of his spine.[266] Stuart suffered great pain as an ambulance took him to Richmond to await his wife's arrival at the home of Dr. Charles Brewer, his brother-in-law. Stuart ordered his sword and spurs be given to his son. His last whispered words were: "I am resigned; God's will be done." He died at 7:38 p.m. on May 12, the following day, before Flora Stuart reached his side. He was 31 years old. Stuart was buried in Richmond's Hollywood Cemetery. Upon learning of Stuart's death, General

Figure 40: *Southern Troopers Song, Dedicated to Gen'l. J. E. B. Stuart and his gallant Soldiers, Sheet music, Danville, Virginia, c. 1864*

Lee is reported to have said that he could hardly keep from weeping at the mere mention of Stuart's name and that Stuart had never given him a bad piece of information.[267]

Flora wore the black of mourning for the remainder of her life, and never remarried. She lived in Saltville, Virginia, for 15 years after the war, where she opened and taught at a school in a log cabin. She worked from 1880 to 1898 as principal of the Virginia Female Institute in Staunton, Virginia, a position for which Robert E. Lee had recommended her before his death ten years earlier.[268] In 1907, the Institute was renamed Stuart Hall School in her honor. Upon the death of her daughter Virginia, from complications in childbirth in 1898, Flora resigned from the Institute and moved to Norfolk, Virginia, where she helped Virginia's widower, Robert Page Waller, in raising her grandchildren. She died in Norfolk on May 10, 1923, after striking her head in a fall on a city sidewalk. She is buried alongside her husband and their daughter, Little Flora, in Hollywood Cemetery in Richmond.[269]

Figure 41: *Stuart's grave in Hollywood Cemetery, Richmond, with temporary marker, 1865*

Legacy and memorials

Like his intimate friend, Stonewall Jackson, General J.E.B. Stuart was a legendary figure and is considered one of the greatest cavalry commanders in American history. His friend from his federal army days, Union Maj. Gen. John Sedgwick, said that Stuart was "the greatest cavalry officer ever foaled in America."[270] Jackson and Stuart, both of whom were killed in battle, had colorful public images, although the latter seems to have been more deliberately crafted. Jeffry D. Wert wrote about Stuart:

> *Stuart had been the Confederacy's knight errant, the bold and dashing cavalier, attired in a resplendent uniform, plumed hat, and cape. Amid a slaughterhouse, he had embodied chivalry, clinging to the pageantry of a long-gone warrior. He crafted the image carefully, and the image befitted him. He saw himself as the Southern people envisaged him. They needed a knight; he needed to be that knight.[271]*

A statue of General J.E.B. Stuart by sculptor Frederick Moynihan was dedicated on Richmond's famed Monument Avenue at Stuart Circle in 1907. Like General Stonewall Jackson, his equestrian statue faces north, indicating that he died in the war. In 1884 the town of Taylorsville, Virginia, was renamed Stuart. The British Army named two models of American-made World War

Figure 42: *Gravesite of Jeb and Flora Stuart, Hollywood Cemetery*

Figure 43: *M3 Stuart tank*

Figure 44: *J.E.B. Stuart statue on Monument Avenue, Richmond, VA, unveiled May 30, 1907*

II tanks, the M3 and M5, the Stuart tank in General Stuart's honor. A high school on Munson's Hill in Falls Church, Virginia and a middle school in Jacksonville, Florida are named for him.[272]

In December 2006, a personal Confederate battle flag, sewn by Flora Stuart, was sold in a Heritage Auction for a world-record price for any Confederate flag, for $956,000 (including buyer's premium).[273] The 34-inch by 34-inch flag was hand-sewn for Stuart by Flora in 1862 and Stuart carried it into some of his most famous battles. Stuart's birthplace, Laurel Hill, located in Patrick County, Virginia, was purchased by the J.E.B. Stuart Birthplace Preservation Trust, Inc., in 1992 to preserve and interpret it.[274]

In popular culture

Comics

- In the long-running comic book *G.I. Combat*, featuring "The Haunted Tank", published by DC Comics from the 1960s through the late 1980s, the ghost of General Stuart guided a tank crew (the tank being, at first, a Stuart, later a Sherman) commanded by his namesake, Lt. Jeb Stuart.[275]

Figure 45: *Another view of the J.E.B. Stuart statue on Monument Avenue in Richmond, Virginia*

Films

- Joseph Fuqua played Stuart in the films *Gettysburg* and *Gods and Generals*.[276]
- Errol Flynn played Stuart in the movie *Santa Fe Trail*, depicting his antebellum life, confronting John Brown in Kansas and at Harper's Ferry. The movie has become infamous for its many historical inaccuracies, one of which was that Stuart, George Armstrong Custer (portrayed by Ronald Reagan in the film), and Philip Sheridan were firm friends and all attended West Point together in 1854.

Literature

- Stuart, along with his warhorse Skylark, is featured prominently in the novel *Traveller* by Richard Adams.[277]
- In the alternate history novel *Gray Victory* (1988), author Robert Skimin depicts Stuart surviving his wound from the battle of Yellow Tavern. After the war, in which the Confederacy emerges victorious, he faces a court of inquiry over his actions at the Battle of Gettysburg.[278]
- In Harry Turtledove's alternate-history novel *How Few Remain* , Stuart is the commanding Confederate general in charge of the occupation and

defense of the recently purchased Mexican provinces of Sonora and Chihuahua in 1881. This is the first volume of the Southern Victory series, where the USA and CSA fight each other repeatedly in the 19th and 20th centuries. Stuart's son and grandson also appear in these novels.[279]

- Several short stories in Barry Hannah's collection *Airships* feature Stuart as a character.
- Stuart's route to Gettysburg is the impetus for the sci-fi-ish book "An End to Bugling" by Edmund G. Love.
- Stuart is also a character in L.M. Elliott's *Annie, Between the States*.
- J.E.B. Stuart is a character in the historical adventure novel *Flashman and the Angel of the Lord* by George Macdonald Fraser featuring Stuart's early-career role in the US Army at abolitionist John Brown's raid on Harper's Ferry.

Music

- "When I Was On Horseback," a song on the folk group Arborea's album *Fortress of the Sun* (2013), features lyrics that refer to Stuart's death near Richmond, Virginia.[280]

References

- Bonekemper, Edward H., III. *How Robert E. Lee Lost the Civil War*. Fredericksburg, VA: Sergeant Kirkland's Press, 1998. ISBN 1-887901-15-9.
- Coddington, Edwin B. *The Gettysburg Campaign; a study in command*. New York: Scribner's, 1968. ISBN 978-0-684-84569-2.
- Davis, Burke. *Jeb Stuart: The Last Cavalier*. New York: Random House, 1957. ISBN 0-517-18597-0.
- Eicher, John H., and David J. Eicher. *Civil War High Commands*. Stanford, CA: Stanford University Press, 2001. ISBN 978-0-8047-3641-1.
- Longacre, Edward G. *The Cavalry at Gettysburg: A Tactical Study of Mounted Operations during the Civil War's Pivotal Campaign, 9 June–14 July, 1863*. Lincoln: University of Nebraska Press, 1986. ISBN 978-0-8032-7941-4.
- Longacre, Edward G. *Lee's Cavalrymen: A History of the Mounted Forces of the Army of Northern Virginia*. Mechanicsburg, PA: Stackpole Books, 2002. ISBN 978-0-8117-0898-2.
- Perry, Thomas D. *J. E. B. Stuart's Birthplace: The History of the Laurel Hill Farm*. Ararat, VA: Laurel Hill Publishing, 2008. ISBN 978-1-4382-3934-7.

- Peterson, Alexander Duncan Campbell. *Schools Across Frontiers: The Story of the International Baccalaureate and the United World Colleges.* La Salle, IL: Open Court Publishing, 2003. ISBN 0-8126-9505-4.
- Rhea, Gordon C. *The Battles for Spotsylvania Court House and the Road to Yellow Tavern, May 7–12, 1864.* Baton Rouge: Louisiana State University Press, 1997. ISBN 978-0-8071-2136-8.
- Robertson, James I., Jr. *Stonewall Jackson: The Man, The Soldier, The Legend.* New York: Simon & Schuster Macmillan, 1997. ISBN 978-0-02-864685-5.
- Salmon, John S. *The Official Virginia Civil War Battlefield Guide.* Mechanicsburg, PA: Stackpole Books, 2001. ISBN 978-0-8117-2868-3.
- Sears, Stephen W. *Chancellorsville.* Boston: Houghton Mifflin, 1996. ISBN 0-395-87744-X.
- Sears, Stephen W. *Gettysburg.* Boston: Houghton Mifflin, 2003. ISBN 0-395-86761-4.
- Sifakis, Stewart. *Who Was Who in the Civil War.* New York: Facts On File, 1988. ISBN 978-0-8160-1055-4.
- Smith, Derek. *The Gallant Dead: Union & Confederate Generals Killed in the Civil War.* Mechanicsburg, PA: Stackpole Books, 2005. ISBN 0-8117-0132-8.
- Starr, Steven. *The Union Cavalry in the Civil War: The War in the East from Gettysburg to Appomattox, 1863–1865.* Volume 2. Baton Rouge: Louisiana State University Press, 2007. Originally published 1981. ISBN 978-0-8071-3292-0.
- Thomas, Emory M. *Bold Dragoon: The Life of J.E.B. Stuart.* Norman: University of Oklahoma Press, 1986. ISBN 978-0-8061-3193-1.
- Warner, Ezra J. *Generals in Gray: Lives of the Confederate Commanders.* Baton Rouge: Louisiana State University Press, 1959. ISBN 978-0-8071-0823-9.
- Wert, Jeffry D. *Cavalryman of the Lost Cause: A Biography of J.E.B. Stuart.* New York: Simon & Schuster, 2008. ISBN 978-0-7432-7819-5.
- Wittenberg, Eric J., and J. David Petruzzi. *Plenty of Blame to Go Around: Jeb Stuart's Controversial Ride to Gettysburg.* New York: Savas Beatie, 2006. ISBN 978-1-932714-20-3.

Further reading

- Brown, Kent Masterson. *Retreat from Gettysburg: Lee, Logistics, & the Pennsylvania Campaign.* Chapel Hill: University of North Carolina Press, 2005. ISBN 978-0-8078-2921-9.
- Laino, Philip, *Gettysburg Campaign Atlas.* 2nd ed. Dayton, OH: Gatehouse Press 2009. ISBN 978-1-934900-45-1.

- McClellan, H B. *The Life and Campaigns of Major-General J.E.B. Stuart: Commander of the Cavalry of the Army of Northern Virginia.*[281] Boston: Houghton, Mifflin and Company, 1885.
- McClellan, Henry B. *I Rode with Jeb Stuart: The Life and Campaigns of Maj. Gen. Jeb Stuart.* Edited by Burke Davis. New York: Da Capo Press, 1994. ISBN 978-0-306-80605-6. First published 1958 by Indiana University Press.
- Mosby, John Singleton. *Mosby's Reminiscences and Stuart's Cavalry Campaigns*[282]. New York: Dodd, Mead & Company, 1887. OCLC 26692400[283].
- Perry, Thomas D. *Laurel Hill Teachers' Guide*[284], 2005.
- Petruzzi, J. David, and Steven Stanley. *The Complete Gettysburg Guide.* New York: Savas Beatie, 2009. ISBN 978-1-932714-63-0.
- Wittenberg, Eric J., J. David Petruzzi, and Michael F. Nugent. *One Continuous Fight: The Retreat from Gettysburg and the Pursuit of Lee's Army of Northern Virginia, July 4-14, 1863.* New York: Savas Beatie, 2008. ISBN 978-1-932714-43-2.

External links

Wikisource has the text of the 1911 *Encyclopædia Britannica* article *Stuart, James Ewell Brown*.

Wikimedia Commons has media related to *James Ewell Brown Stuart*.

- Laurel Hill – Stuart's Birthplace[285]
- J. E. B. Stuart[286] at *Find a Grave*
- J. E. B. Stuart in *Encyclopedia Virginia*[287]

Gouverneur K. Warren

Gouverneur Kemble Warren	
Nick-name(s)	Hero of Little Round Top
Born	January 8, 1830 Cold Spring, New York
Died	August 8, 1882 (aged 52) Newport, Rhode Island
Place of burial	Island Cemetery, Newport, Rhode Island
Alle-giance	United States
Service/-branch	United States Army Union Army
Years of service	1850–1882
Rank	★★★ Major general
Com-mands held	5th New York Volunteer Infantry II Corps V Corps

Battles/-wars	American Civil War
	• Peninsula Campaign
	• Battle of Fredericksburg
	• Battle of Chancellorsville
	• Battle of Gettysburg
	• Battle of Bristoe Station
	• Overland Campaign
	  • Battle of the Wilderness
	• Siege of Petersburg
	• Appomattox Campaign
	  • Battle of Five Forks

Gouverneur Kemble Warren (January 8, 1830 – August 8, 1882) was a civil engineer and Union Army general during the American Civil War. He is best remembered for arranging the last-minute defense of Little Round Top during the Battle of Gettysburg and is often referred to as the "Hero of Little Round Top." His subsequent service as a corps commander and his remaining military career were ruined during the Battle of Five Forks, when he was relieved of command of the V Corps by Philip Sheridan, who claimed that Warren had moved too slowly.

Early life

Warren was born in Cold Spring, Putnam County, New York, and named for Gouverneur Kemble, a prominent local Congressman, diplomat, industrialist, and owner of the West Point Foundry. His sister, Emily Warren Roebling, would later play a significant role in the building of the Brooklyn Bridge. He entered the United States Military Academy at age 16 and graduated second in his class of 44 cadets in 1850.[288] He was commissioned a brevet second lieutenant in the Corps of Topographical Engineers. In the antebellum years he worked on the Mississippi River, on transcontinental railroad surveys, and mapped the trans-Mississippi West. He served as the engineer on William S. Harney's Battle of Ash Hollow in the Nebraska Territory in 1855, where he saw his first combat.[289,290]

He took part in studies of possible transcontinental railroad routes, creating the first comprehensive map of the United States west of the Mississippi in 1857. This required extensive explorations of the vast Nebraska Territory, including Nebraska, North Dakota, South Dakota, part of Montana, and part of Wyoming.

One region he surveyed was the Minnesota River Valley, a valley much larger than what would be expected from the low-flow Minnesota River. In some places the valley is 5 miles (8 km) wide and 250 feet (80 m) deep. Warren first explained the hydrology of the region in 1868, attributing the gorge to a massive river, which drained Lake Agassiz between 11,700 and 9,400 years ago. The great river was named glacial River Warren in his honor after his death.

Civil War

At the start of the war, Warren was a first lieutenant and mathematics instructor at the United States Military Academy at West Point, across the Hudson River from his hometown. He helped raise a local regiment for service in the Union Army and was appointed lieutenant colonel of the 5th New York Infantry on May 14, 1861. Warren and his regiment saw their first combat at the Battle of Big Bethel in Virginia on June 10, arguably the first major land engagement of

Figure 46: *Commanders of the Army of the Potomac, Gouverneur K. Warren, William H. French, George G. Meade, Henry J. Hunt, Andrew A. Humphreys and George Sykes in September 1863.*

the war. He was promoted to colonel and regimental commander on September 10.

In the 1862 Peninsula Campaign, Warren commanded his regiment at the Siege of Yorktown and also assisted the chief topographical engineer of the Army of the Potomac, Brig. Gen. Andrew A. Humphreys, by leading reconnaissance missions and drawing detailed maps of appropriate routes for the army in its advance up the Virginia Peninsula. He commanded a brigade (3rd Brigade, 2nd Division, V Corps) during the Seven Days Battles and was wounded in the knee at the Battle of Gaines' Mill, although he refused to be taken from the field. At the Battle of Malvern Hill, his brigade stopped the attack of a Confederate division. He continued to lead the brigade at the Second Battle of Bull Run, suffering heavy casualties in a heroic stand against an overwhelming enemy assault,[291] and at Antietam, where the V Corps was in reserve and saw no combat.

Warren was promoted to brigadier general on September 26, 1862, and he and his brigade fought in the Battle of Fredericksburg in December. When Maj. Gen. Joseph Hooker reorganized the Army of the Potomac in February 1863, he named Warren his chief topographical engineer and then chief engineer.

As chief engineer, Warren was commended for his service in the Battle of Chancellorsville.

At the start of the Gettysburg Campaign, as Confederate General Robert E. Lee began his invasion of Pennsylvania, Warren advised Hooker on the routes the Army should take in pursuit. On the second day of the Battle of Gettysburg, July 2, 1863, Warren initiated the defense of Little Round Top, recognizing the importance of the undefended position on the left flank of the Union Army, and directing, on his own initiative, the brigade of Colonel Strong Vincent to occupy it just minutes before it was attacked. Warren suffered a minor neck wound during the Confederate assault.

Promoted to major general after Gettysburg (August 8, 1863), Warren commanded the II Corps from August 1863 until March 1864, replacing the wounded Maj. Gen. Winfield S. Hancock, and distinguishing himself at the Battle of Bristoe Station. On March 13, 1865, he was brevetted to major general in the regular army for his actions at Bristoe Station. During the Mine Run Campaign, Warren's corps was ordered to attack Lee's army, but he perceived that a trap had been laid and refused the order from army commander Maj. Gen. George G. Meade. Although initially angry at Warren, Meade acknowledged that he had been right. Upon Hancock's return from medical leave, and the spring 1864 reorganization of the Army of the Potomac, Warren assumed command of the V Corps and led it through the Overland Campaign, the Siege of Petersburg, and the Appomattox Campaign.

During these Virginia campaigns, Warren established a reputation of bringing his engineering traits of deliberation and caution to the role of infantry corps commander. He won the Battle of Globe Tavern, August 18 to August 20, 1864, cutting the Weldon Railroad, a vital supply route north to Petersburg. He also won a limited success in the Battle of Peebles' Farm in September 1864, carrying a part of the Confederate lines protecting supplies moving to Petersburg on the Boydton Plank Road.

The aggressive Maj. Gen. Philip Sheridan, a key subordinate of Lt. Gen. Ulysses S. Grant, was dissatisfied with Warren's performance. He was angry at Warren's corps for supposedly obstructing roads after the Battle of the Wilderness and its cautious actions during the Siege of Petersburg. At the beginning of the Appomattox Campaign, Sheridan requested that the VI Corps be assigned to his pursuit of Lee's army, but Grant insisted that the V Corps was better positioned. He gave Sheridan written permission to relieve Warren if he felt it was justified "for the good of the service."[292] Grant later wrote in his *Personal Memoirs*,[293]

I was so much dissatisfied with Warren's dilatory movements in the battle of White Oak Road and in his failure to reach Sheridan in time, that I was

Figure 47: *Gerhardt's statue of Warren on Little Round Top in Gettysburg*

*very much afraid that at the last moment he would fail Sheridan. He was
a man of fine intelligence, great earnestness, quick perception, and could
make his dispositions as quickly as any officer, under difficulties where he
was forced to act. But I had before discovered a defect which was beyond
his control, that was very prejudicial to his usefulness in emergencies like
the one just before us. He could see every danger at a glance before he
had encountered it. He would not only make preparations to meet the
danger which might occur, but he would inform his commanding officer
what others should do while he was executing his move.*

—Ulysses S. Grant, Personal Memoirs

At the Battle of Five Forks on April 1, 1865, Sheridan judged that the V Corps
had moved too slowly into the attack, and criticised Warren fiercely for not
being at the front of his columns. Warren had been held up, searching for
Samuel W. Crawford's division, which had gone astray in the woods. But
overall, he had handled his corps efficiently, and their attack had carried the
day at Five Forks, arguably the pivotal battle of the final days. Nevertheless,
Sheridan relieved Warren of command on the spot.[294] He was assigned to
the defenses of Petersburg and then briefly to command of the Department of
Mississippi.

Postbellum career

Humiliated by Sheridan, Warren resigned his commission as major general of volunteers in protest on May 27, 1865, reverting to his permanent rank as major in the Corps of Engineers. He served as an engineer for seventeen years, building railroads, with assignments along the Mississippi River, achieving the rank of lieutenant colonel in 1879. But the career that had shown so much promise at Gettysburg was ruined. He urgently requested a court of inquiry to exonerate him from the stigma of Sheridan's action. Numerous requests were ignored or refused until Ulysses S. Grant retired from the presidency. President Rutherford B. Hayes ordered a court of inquiry that convened in 1879 and, after hearing testimony from dozens of witnesses over 100 days, found that Sheridan's relief of Warren had been unjustified. Unfortunately for Warren, these results were not published until after his death.[295]

Warren's last assignment in the Army was as district engineer for Newport, Rhode Island, where he died in 1882. He was buried in the Island Cemetery in Newport in civilian clothes and without military honors at his own request. His last words were, "The flag! The flag!"[296]

In memoriam

A bronze statue of Warren stands on Little Round Top in Gettysburg National Military Park. It was created by Karl Gerhardt (1853–1940) and dedicated in 1888. Another bronze statue, by Henry Baerer (1837–1908), was erected in the Grand Army Plaza, Brooklyn, New York. It depicts Warren standing in uniform, with field binoculars on a granite pedestal, made of stone quarried at Little Round Top.

Reflecting a pattern of naming many Washington, DC streets in newly developed areas in the Capital after Civil War generals, an east-west street in the Northwest quadrant is named Warren Street, NW.

The G. K. Warren Prize is awarded approximately every four years by the National Academy of Sciences. It is funded by a gift from his daughter, Miss Emily B. Warren, in memory of her father.

References

- Eicher, John H., and David J. Eicher. *Civil War High Commands*. Stanford, CA: Stanford University Press, 2001. ISBN 0-8047-3641-3.
- Grant, Ulysses S. *Personal Memoirs of U. S. Grant*[297]. 2 vols. Charles L. Webster & Company, 1885–86. ISBN 0-914427-67-9.

- Heidler, David S., and Jeanne T. Heidler. "Gouverneur Kemble Warren." In *Encyclopedia of the American Civil War: A Political, Social, and Military History*, edited by David S. Heidler and Jeanne T. Heidler. New York: W. W. Norton & Company, 2000. ISBN 0-393-04758-X.
- Warner, Ezra J. *Generals in Blue: Lives of the Union Commanders*. Baton Rouge: Louisiana State University Press, 1964. ISBN 0-8071-0822-7.
- Wittenberg, Eric J. *Little Phil: A Reassessment of the Civil War Leadership of Gen. Philip H. Sheridan*. Washington, DC: Potomac Books, 2002. ISBN 1-57488-548-0.

Further reading

- Jordan, David M. *"Happiness Is Not My Companion": The Life of General G. K. Warren*. Bloomington: Indiana University Press, 2001. ISBN 978-0-253-10894-4.

External links

 Wikimedia Commons has media related to *Gouverneur K. Warren*.

- Works by or about Gouverneur K. Warren[298] at Internet Archive
- ☺ "Warren, Gouverneur Kemble". *Appletons' Cyclopædia of American Biography*. 1889.

Military offices		
Preceded by **William Hays**	**Commander of the Second Army Corps** August 16, 1863 – August 26, 1863	Succeeded by **John C. Caldwell**
Preceded by **John C. Caldwell**	**Commander of the Second Army Corps** September 2, 1863 – October 10, 1863	Succeeded by **John C. Caldwell**
Preceded by **John C. Caldwell**	**Commander of the Second Army Corps** October 12, 1863 – December 16, 1863	Succeeded by **John C. Caldwell**
Preceded by **John C. Caldwell**	**Commander of the Second Army Corps** December 29, 1863 – January 9, 1864	Succeeded by **John C. Caldwell**
Preceded by **John C. Caldwell**	**Commander of the Second Army Corps** January 15, 1864 – March 24, 1864	Succeeded by **Winfield S. Hancock**
Preceded by **George Sykes**	**Commander of the Fifth Army Corps** March 23, 1864 – January 2, 1865	Succeeded by **Samuel W. Crawford**
Preceded by **Samuel W. Crawford**	**Commander of the Fifth Army Corps** January 27, 1865 – April 1, 1865	Succeeded by **Charles Griffin**

Appendix

References

[1] Coddington, pp. 535–36; Wittenberg et al., p. 39; Brown, pp. 9–11.

[2] Sears, p. 471; Gottfried, p. 278: Imboden claimed that there were 12,000 wounded men in his wagon train.

[3] Wittenberg et al., pp. 28, 29, 36; Coddington, pp. 536–37.

[4] Coddington, pp. 537–38; Gottfried, p. 278; Wittenberg et al., p. 5.

[5] Wittenberg et al., pp. 160–61; Sears, p. 481.

[6] Coddington, p. 569.

[7] Coddington, 557-63.

[8] Brown, pp. 21, 299.

[9] Sears, pp. 532–43.

[10] Longacre, pp. 245–46; Wittenberg et al., pp. 2, 5; Coddington, p. 538; Gottfried, p. 279.

[11] Wittenberg et al., pp. 5–26; Sears, p. 481.

[12] Coddington, p. 539; Gottfried, p. 280; Wittenberg et al., p. 39.

[13] Coddington, pp. 539–40.

[14] Longacre, pp. 235–37.

[15] Wittenberg et al., pp. 152–55; Gottfried, p. 278; Coddington, p. 543.

[16] Coddington, pp. 544–48; Wittenberg et al., pp. 46–47, 79–80; Gottfried, p. 280.

[17] Huntington, pp. 131–33; Wittenberg et al., 49–74; Sears, pp. 480–81; Brown, pp. 128–36, 184; Coddington, p. 548; Gottfried, pp. 278–81; Longacre, pp. 249–50. A historical marker on East Cemetery Hill at Gettysburg Battlefield uses the term "Fight" for the "Monterey Gap" action, Longacre uses "skirmish". All of the other references use the name "Monterey Pass". The number of wagons captured is disputed. Brown reports that local residents cited "400 or 500". Longacre cites sources for 40 (Stuart) and 150 (Union Col. Pennock Huey). Huntington cites 300.

[18] Wittenberg et al., pp. 81–86.

[19] Wittenberg et al., pp. 81–86; Gottfried, p. 280; Coddington, pp. 549–51.

[20] Coddington, p. 552.

[21] Wittenberg et al., pp. 86–89; Coddington, pp. 551–52.

[22] Alexander, Ted, "Battle of Hagerstown bought Lee some time", *Washington Times*, July 3, 1999.

[23] Wittenberg et al., pp. 107–22; Coddington, pp. 552–53; Sears, pp. 482–83; Gottfried, pp. 282–85.

[24] Coddington, pp. 552–53; Sears, pp. 482–83; Gottfried, pp. 282–85.

[25] Wittenberg et al., pp. 173–97; Brown, pp. 290–93.

[26] Wittenberg et al., pp. 167–68, 207–34; Brown, pp. 302–307.

[27] Coddington, p. 554.

[28] Coddington, pp. 555, 556, 564; Wittenberg et al., p. 335.

[29] Woodworth, p. 214.

[30] Coddington, pp. 565–66; Gottfried, p. 286.

[31] Coddington, p. 567; Sears, pp. 488–89; Gottfried, p. 288; Wittenberg et al., pp. 249, 258–62.

[32] Coddington, pp. 569–70; Wittenberg et al., pp. 263–64, 271–74; Gottfried, p. 288.

[33] Sears, pp. 489–92; Gottfried, p. 288; Coddington, pp. 570–71: Lee disputed this large number of prisoners, claiming that he lost only a small number of stragglers.

[34] Sears, p. 493; Woodworth, p. 217.

[35] Wittenberg et al., p. xix.

[36] Kennedy, p. 213; Wittenberg et al., p. 345.

[37] Salmon, pp. 215–16; Kennedy, pp. 213–14; Eicher, p. 596; Wittenberg et al., pp. 345–46.

[38] Wittenberg et al., pp. 343–44.

[39] Wittenberg et al., p. 343.

[40] Sears, pp. 496, 498.

[41] Wittenberg et al., p. 347.

[42] Eicher, pp. 597–98, 618–19; Wittenberg et al., pp. 342–43.

[43] //www.worldcat.org/oclc/5890637

[44] http://www.dean.usma.edu/history/web03/atlases/american_civil_war/

[45] http://www.bibliobase.com/history/readerscomp/civwar/html/cw_000106_entries.htm

[46] http://www.cr.nps.gov/hps/abpp/battles/bycampgn.htm#East63

[47] http://www.historyanimated.com/Gettysburgh.html

[48] Longacre, p. 236, indicates that the 6th Virginia conducted the second charge alone.

[49] http://members.tripod.com/k_lucier/platt.htm

[50] Brown, p. 128; Huntington, p. 132.

[51] Brown, p. 143.

[52] Huntington, pp. 131-33; Wittenberg et al., 49-74; Sears, pp. 480-81; Brown, pp. 128-36, 184; Coddington, p. 548; Gottfried, pp. 278-81; Longacre, pp. 249-50. A historical marker on East Cemetery Hill at Gettysburg Battlefield uses the term "Fight" for the "Monterey Gap" action, Longacre uses "skirmish". All of the other references use the name "Monterey Pass".

[53] Coddington, pp. 536-38; Wittenberg et al., pp. 1-6.

[54] Coddington, pp. 537-39; Gottfried, pp. 278-80; Wittenberg et al., pp. 5, 39.

[55] Wittenberg et al., pp. 49-50.

[56] Brown, pp. 124, 130; Wittenberg et al., pp. 52-54; Gottfried, p. 278; Coddington, p. 543.

[57] Wittenberg et al., pp. 50-52; Brown, p. 127.

[58] Wittenberg et al., pp. 54-58; Brown, p. 131.

[59] Wittenberg et al., pp. 59-60; Brown, pp. 124, 130-32.

[60] Brown, pp. 133-34; Wittenberg et al., pp. 60-61.

[61] Wittenberg et al., pp. 62-64.

[62] Brown, pp. 135-37; Wittenberg et al., pp. 64-66.

[63] Wittenberg et al., pp. 66-69.

[64] Huntington, pp. 131-33; Wittenberg et al., 49-74; Sears, pp. 480-81; Brown, pp. 142, 144, 184; Coddington, p. 548; Gottfried, pp. 278-81; Longacre, pp. 249-50. The number of wagons captured is disputed. Brown reports that local residents cited "400 or 500". Longacre cites sources for 40 (Stuart) and 150 (Union Col. Pennock Huey). Huntington cites 300.

[65] Wittenberg et al., pp. 81-86.

[66] Coddington, pp. 550-74.

[67] http://www.therecordherald.com/features/x2022446673/Battle-of-Monterey-Pass-documentary-by-Historical-Entertainment-premieres-Saturday-March-12?zc_p=0

[68] http://www.emmitsburg.net/archive_list/articles/history/civil_war/the_battle_of_monterey.htm

[69] http://www.emmitsburg.net/montereypass/index.htm

[70] http://www.montereypassbattlefield.org/

[71] //tools.wmflabs.org/geohack/geohack.php?pagename=Battle_of_Williamsport&params=39_38_N_77_43_W_type:event_region:US-MD

[72] http://www.nps.gov/abpp/battles/md004.htm

[73] //tools.wmflabs.org/geohack/geohack.php?pagename=Battle_of_Boonsboro&params=39.5254_N_-77.6632_E_type:event_region:US-MD

[74] Maryland Civil War Trails wayside marker for the Battle of Boonsboro http://www.hmdb.org/marker.asp?marker=1630

[75] http://www.nps.gov/history/hps/abpp/battles/md006.htm

[76] Maryland Civil War Trails wayside marker for the Battle of Funkstown http://www.hmdb.org/marker.asp?marker=1158

[77] Maryland Historical Society's marker for the Battle of Funkstown http://www.hmdb.org/Marker.asp?Marker=388

[78] http://www.hmdb.org/marker.asp?marker=1158

[79] //tools.wmflabs.org/geohack/geohack.php?pagename=Battle_of_Funkstown&params=39.60592_N_-77.700462_E_type:event_region:US-MD

[80] Kennedy, pp. 213-14.

[81] Salmon, pp. 215–16.

[82] http://www.nps.gov/history/hps/abpp/battles/va108.htm

[83] //tools.wmflabs.org/geohack/geohack.php?pagename=Battle_of_Manassas_Gap&params=38. 914_N_78.114_W_type:event_region:US_scale:30000

[84] See Aftermath.

[85] Salmon, p. 218.

[86] Kennedy, pp. 252-55. The total casualties are the sum of First Auburn (50 total on both sides), Second Auburn (113 total), Bristoe Station (540 Union, 1380 Confederate), Buckland Mills (230 total), and Second Rappahannock Station (461 Union, 2,041 Confederate, of which 1,973 were captured).

[87] NPS Auburn I http://www.nps.gov/history/hps/abpp/battles/va039.htm

[88] NPS Auburn II http://www.nps.gov/history/hps/abpp/battles/va041.htm

[89] NPS Bristoe Station http://www.nps.gov/history/hps/abpp/battles/va040.htm

[90] NPS Buckland Mills http://www.nps.gov/history/hps/abpp/battles/va042.htm

[91] NPS Rappahannock Station II http://www.nps.gov/history/hps/abpp/battles/va043.htm

[92] Salmon, pp. 224-25.

[93] http://www.cr.nps.gov/hps/abpp/battles/bycampgn.htm#East63

[94] http://emergingcivilwar.com/2013/12/03/i-would-save-him-the-trouble-robert-e-lees-struggle-of-supply-in-the-fall-1863campaign/#more-10359

[95] http://www.cr.nps.gov/hps/abpp/battles/va039.htm

[96] http://www.nps.gov/hps/abpp/CWSII/VirginiaBattlefieldProfiles/Aldie%20to%20Auburn%20II.pdf

[97] //tools.wmflabs.org/geohack/geohack.php?pagename=First_Battle_of_Auburn&params=38. 7_N_77.7_W_

[98] //tools.wmflabs.org/geohack/geohack.php?pagename=Second_Battle_of_Auburn&params= 38.70213_N_77.70181_W_

[99] http://www.cr.nps.gov/hps/abpp/battles/va041.htm

[100] http://www.nps.gov/hps/abpp/CWSII/VirginiaBattlefieldProfiles/Aldie%20to%20Auburn%20II.pdf

[101] //tools.wmflabs.org/geohack/geohack.php?pagename=Battle_of_Bristoe_Station&params=38. 7234_N_77.5418_W_region:US-VA_type:event_scale:50000

[102] Kennedy, p. 254, cites Union losses of about 540, Confederate about 1,380. Salmon, p. 236, cites total casualties of 1,80, "all but 550 Confederate." Jordan, p. 108, cites casualties for Warren as 350, for Heth 1,360 killed or wounded and 450 captured.

[103] Jordan, p. 106.

[104] Jordan, pp. 106–107.

[105] Jordan, pp. 107–108.

[106] Jordan, p. 108.

[107] Walker, pp. 321–360.

[108] Freeman, vol. 3, pp. 326–27.

[109] Jordan, p. 110.

[110] Freeman, vol. 3, p. 327.

[111] http://www.nps.gov/abpp/battles/va040.htm

[112] http://www.nps.gov/abpp/CWSII/VirginiaBattlefieldProfiles/Blackburns%20Ford%20to%20Buckland%20Mills.pdf

[113] https://archive.org/details/historyofseconda01walk

[114] //www.worldcat.org/oclc/287902026

[115] http://encyclopediavirginia.org/Bristoe_Station_Battle_of

[116] http://www.pwcgov.org/default.aspx?topic=010014001370005130

[117] http://civilwardailygazette.com/2013/10/14/to-halt-was-to-await-annihilation-lee-lets-meade-slip-away/#comment-509512

[118] http://emergingcivilwar.com/2013/10/14/swapped-identities-battle-of-bristoe-station-october-14-1863/

[119] http://www.civilwar.org/battlefields/bristoestation/bristoe-station-history-articles/bristoecampi.html

[120] http://www.cr.nps.gov/hps/abpp/battles/va042.htm

[121] http://www.nps.gov/hps/abpp/CWSII/VirginiaBattlefieldProfiles/Blackburns%20Ford%20to%20Buckland%20Mills.pdf

[122] //tools.wmflabs.org/geohack/geohack.php?pagename=Battle_of_Buckland_Mills&params=
38.7747_N_-77.692_E_type:event_region:US-VA

[123]

[124] http://www.nps.gov/frsp/rapp.htm

[125] http://www.cr.nps.gov/hps/abpp/battles/va043.htm

[126] http://www.nps.gov/hps/abpp/CWSII/VirginiaBattlefieldProfiles/Rappahannock%20I%
20and%20II.pdf

[127] //tools.wmflabs.org/geohack/geohack.php?pagename=Second_Battle_of_Rappahannock_
Station&params=38.5330_N_-77.8136_E_region:US_type:event_scale:10000

[128] Esposito, map 119.

[129] NPS http://www.cr.nps.gov/hps/abpp/battles/va044.htm

[130] http://www.essentialcivilwarcurriculum.com/the-mine-run-campaign.html

[131] //www.worldcat.org/oclc/5890637

[132] http://www.dean.usma.edu/history/web03/atlases/american_civil_war/

[133] http://www.nps.gov/abpp/battles/va044.htm

[134] http://encyclopediavirginia.org/Mine_Run_Campaign

[135] //tools.wmflabs.org/geohack/geohack.php?pagename=Battle_of_Mine_Run&params=38.
3379_N_-77.8187_E_region:US_type:event_scale:10000

[136] Florida History Quarterly http//fulltext10.fcla.edu

[137] John French Conklin bio http://www.militariamuseum.com/collection/Conklin/ConklinBio.
htm

[138] https://web.archive.org/web/20080208215607/http://www.generalsandbrevets.com/ngf/
french.htm

[139] Dupuy, Trevor N., Curt Johnson, and David L. Bongard. *The Harper Encyclopedia of Military
Biography*. New York: HarperCollins, 1992, p. 363. ISBN 978-0-06-270015-5.

[140] Staunton Artillery, First Bull Run http://www.firstbullrun.co.uk/Shenandoah/Third%
20Brigade/staunton-artillery.html

[141] Virginia Light Artillery (Staunton Artillery) http://www.nps.gov/civilwar/search-battle-units-
detail.htm?battleUnitCode=CVAGARBCAL, *National Park Service*

[142] Eicher, John H., and David J. Eicher. *Civil War High Commands*. Stanford, CA: Stanford
University Press, 2001, p. 363. ISBN 0-8047-3641-3.

[143] *The War of the Rebellion: a Compilation of the Official Records of the Union and Confederate
Armies* http://ebooks.library.cornell.edu/m/moawar/waro.html, *Cornell University Library*

[144] Imboden, John D. *The Coal and Iron Resources of Virginia: Their Extent, Commercial Value,
and Early Development Considered. A Paper Read Before a Meeting of Members of the Legislature and Prominent Citizens in the Capitol at Richmond, February 19th, 1872.* Richmond:
Clemmitt & Jones, printers, 1872.

[145] Brief History of Damascus, Virginia http://www.visitdamascus.org/history-of-damascus/

[146] John D. Imboden's Obituary, *Staunton Vindicator*, 23 August 23, 1895.

[147] John D. Imboden http://www.hollywoodcemetery.org/john-d-imboden, *The Hollywood Cemetery*

[148]

[149] Woodward, Harold R. *Defender of the Valley: Brigadier General John Daniel Imboden, CSA*.
http://www.allofsouthamerica.com/bks_RPC/defender.htm Berryville, VA: Rockbridge Publ.,
1996.

[150] https://books.google.com/books?id=jdN4WS1JbEEC&lpg=PA68&ots=XcoH6sMkNN&dq=
the%20Staunton%20Artillery&pg=PA6#v=onepage&q&f=false

[151] https://www.findagrave.com/cgi-bin/fg.cgi?page=gr&GRid=4658

[152] http://www.hollywoodcemetery.org/john-d-imboden

[153] Eicher, pp. 325-6.

[154] Eicher, p. 326.

[155] McClure, Alexander K., ed., *The Annals of the Civil War Written by Leading Participants North
and South*, Philadelphia: Times Publishing Company, 1879, p. 173.

[156] 'maps.google.com Grumble Jones Ct. Centreville, VA 20121' http://www.google.com/search?
q=grumble+jones+court+centreville+va&ie=utf-8&oe=utf-8&aq=t&rls Retrieved February 2,
2012.

[157] http://www.rocemabra.com/~roger/tagg/generals/

[158] http://www.dixiebeeliners.com/index.html

[159] http://www.google.com/search?q=grumble+jones+court+centreville+va&ie=utf-8&oe=utf-8&aq=t&rls

[160] http://www.gdg.org/Research/OOB/Confederate/July1-3/wjones.html

[161] https://www.findagrave.com/cgi-bin/fg.cgi?page=gr&GRid=11004

[162] http://www.geni.com/people/Luisa-Valdivieso-Ar%C3%A1oz/6000000010062152360

[163] https://familysearch.org/ark:/61903/1:1:24CP-21P

[164] Battery Kilpatrick at Junglefighter.com http://junglefighter.panamanow.net/html/Kilpatrick.htm

[165] Fort Sherman at NorthAmericanForts.com http://www.northamericanforts.com/East/cz.html

[166] //www.worldcat.org/oclc/45917117

[167] http://ehistory.osu.edu/osu/books/battles/index.cfm

[168] //www.worldcat.org/oclc/2048818

[169] //www.worldcat.org/oclc/497732

[170] //www.worldcat.org/oclc/42428710

[171] //www.worldcat.org/oclc/11893938

[172] //www.worldcat.org/oclc/53405397

[173] //www.worldcat.org/oclc/14075041

[174] //www.worldcat.org/oclc/1881547

[175] http://www.rocemabra.com/~roger/tagg/generals/

[176] //www.worldcat.org/oclc/39725526

[177] http://www.gdg.org/Research/OOB/Union/July1-3/jkilpatr.html

[178] Berthrong, pp. 133-40; Grinnell, pp. 111-21.

[179] A Sedgwick Genealogy: Descendants of Deacon Benjamin Sedgwick http://sedgwick.org/na/library/books/sed1961/sed1961-100.html

[180] http://www.civilwar.org/education/history/biographies/john-sedgwick-1.html

[181] Foote, p. 203.

[182] According to Rhea, the preeminent historian of the Overland Campaign, pp. 93-96, there is no record of the identity or location of the sharpshooter. Union troops from the 6th Vermont claim to have shot an unidentified sharpshooter as they crossed the fields seeking revenge. Ben Powell of the 12th South Carolina claimed credit, although his account has been discounted because the general he shot at with a Whitworth rifled musket was mounted, probably Brig Gen. William H. Morris. Thomas Burgess of the 15th South Carolina has also been cited by some veterans.

[183] Rhea, p. 95.

[184] Fort Hell http://www.craterroad.com/forthell.html. The Civil War Siege of Petersburg

[185] Sedgwick County https://coloradowest.auraria.edu/newspaper-histories/sedgwick-county. Center for Colorado and the West at Auraria Library

[186] //www.worldcat.org/oclc/254915143

[187] //www.worldcat.org/oclc/419857

[188] http://www.civilwarhome.com/sedgwickdeath.htm

[189] http://www.civilwarhome.com/sedgwickbio.htm

[190] http://www.civil-war-tribute.com/aop-John-Sedgwick-bio.html

[191] http://members.skyweb.net/~channy/scdgwick.html

[192] https://www.findagrave.com/cgi-bin/fg.cgi?page=gr&GRid=6475

[193] Eicher, pp. 517–18.

[194] Thomas, p. 151; Davis, p. 237.

[195] Donald R. Jermann, *Civil War Battlefield Orders Gone Awry: The Written Word and Its Consequences in 13 Engagements* (McFarland, 2012) p. 129.

[196] Life of Jeb Stuart by Mary Williamson. Christian Liberty Press, Jan 1, 1997 page 1

[197] Wert, pp. 5–6, lists the children as Nancy Anne Dabney, born in 1818, Bethenia Pannill in 1819, Mary Tucker in 1821, David Pannill in 1823, William Alexander in 1826, John Dabney in 1828, Columbia Lafayette in 1830, James in 1833, an unnamed son who died at the age of three months in 1834, Virginia Josephine in 1836, and Victoria Augusta in 1838. Thomas, p. 7, claims that James was the youngest son of ten [unnamed] children.

[198] Thomas, p. 5.

[199] Wert, p. 5.

[200] Thomas, pp. 11–12; Wert, p. 8.
[201] Wert, p. 10.
[202] Wert, p. 11; Davis, p. 19.
[203] Thomas, p. 18.
[204] Davis, p. 33; Wert, p. 15.
[205] Wert, p. 18.
[206] Thomas, pp. 18–32; Davis, p. 27.
[207] Wert, pp. 22–23.
[208] Thomas, pp. 40–41.
[209] Wert, p. 25.
[210] Davis, p. 36.
[211] Thomas, pp. 41–43; Davis, p. 37; Wert, pp. 26–29.
[212] Wert, pp. 30–31.
[213] Davis, p. 40; Wert, pp. 33–35.
[214] Wert, p. 35.
[215] Wert, pp. 37–39.
[216] Wert, pp. 45, 52; Davis, pp. 47–40.
[217] Thomas, p. 95.
[218] Wert, pp. 42, 76.
[219] Wert, p. 49; Davis, pp. 51–52.
[220] Wert, p. 62.
[221] Wert, pp. 93–101; Davis, pp. 111–30.
[222] Wert, pp. 125–29; Davis, pp. 167–72.
[223] Wert, pp. 136–37; Davis, pp. 183–84.
[224] Wert, p. 144.
[225] Wert, pp. 147–50.
[226] Wert, pp. 156–58; Davis, pp. 205–06.
[227] Robertson, p. 235.
[228] Wert, pp. 167–76; Thomas, pp. 173–80; Davis, pp. 215–37.
[229] Robertson, pp. 653–54; Thomas, pp. 172–73.
[230] Wert, pp. 179–83.
[231] Wert, pp. 190–93; Davis, pp. 253–58.
[232] Wert, pp. 195–98; Davis, pp. 261–63.
[233] Longacre, Lee's Cavalrymen, pp. 169–74; Wert, pp. 207–10, 321; Davis, pp. 267–76; Thomas, p. 270.
[234] Wert, pp. 222–31; Davis, pp. 290–98.
[235] Sears, Chancellorsville, p. 325.
[236] Wert, p. 233.
[237] Sears, Gettysburg, pp. 62–63.
[238] Longacre, Cavalry at Gettysburg, pp. 39–40; Sears, Gettysburg, pp. 62–64; Wert, pp. 238–39.
[239] Longacre, Cavalry at Gettysburg, pp. 40–41; Sears, Gettysburg, pp. 62–64.
[240] Salmon, p. 193; Wert, p. 239.
[241] Salmon, p. 198; Wert, p. 240.
[242] Salmon, pp. 199–203; Wert, pp. 241–48; Davis, pp. 305–12.
[243] Wert, p. 251.
[244] Longacre, Cavalry at Gettysburg, pp. 65–86; Wert, pp. 249–52.
[245] Sears, Gettysburg, pp. 104–06; Longacre, pp. 148–52; Gottfried, p. 28; Coddington, p. 108.
[246] Coddington, pp. 108–13; Longacre, pp. 152–53; Sears, Gettysburg, p. 106; Gottfried, p. 28.
[247] Wittenberg and Petruzzi, pp. 19–32; Longacre, pp. 154–56; Sears, Gettysburg, pp. 106, 130–31.
[248] Coddington, pp. 199–200; Longacre, pp. 156–58; Wittenberg and Petruzzi, pp. 47–64.
[249] Coddington, pp. 200–01; Wittenberg and Petruzzi, pp. 65–117; Longacre, pp. 161, 172–79.
[250] Wittenberg and Petruzzi, pp. 139–78; Longacre, pp. 193–202.
[251] Sears, Gettysburg, pp. 257–58. Longacre, pp. 215–16, argues that a bitter confrontation never took place.
[252] Longacre, Cavalry at Gettysburg, pp. 220–31.

253 Longacre, *Lee's Cavalrymen*, pp. 223–37; Wert, pp. 292–98.

254 Wert, p. 300.

255 Coddington, p. 207.

256 Wittenberg and Petruzzi, pp. 219–28.

257 Longacre, *Lee's Cavalrymen*, pp. 215–16; Longacre, *Cavalry at Gettysburg*, p. 271; Coddington, pp. 205–08; Wittenberg and Petruzzi, pp. 263–98; Wert, pp. 299–302.

258 Bonekemper, p. 139.

259 Wert, pp. 308–09.

260 Wert, pp. 320–21.

261 Wert, pp. 313–21; Davis, pp. 360–67.

262 Wert, pp. 338–46; Davis, pp. 378–84.

263 Wert, p. 346; Davis, p. 384.

264 Wert, pp. 346–49.

265 Smith, p. 242; Salmon, p. 283; Starr, p. 107; Rhea, pp. 209, 390; Thomas, p. 292; Edward G. Longacre, writing in a June 2004 *Civil War Times* article http://www.historynet.com/wars_conflicts/american_civil_war/3027331.html?page=3&c=y, claims that Huff's shot was from away, an arguably impressive feat with a pistol; in his book, *Lincoln's Cavalrymen* (p. 268), Longacre states that Huff was able to advance "close enough" to Stuart to shoot him in the abdomen, although he was not aware at the time that his victim was Stuart. Private Huff was killed a month later at the Battle of Haw's Shop. Wert, pp. 347–58, disputes the possibility that Huff fired the mortal shot, stating that the evidence points to an unnamed trooper in either the 1st or 7th Michigan.

266 Smith, p. 357.

267 Smith, p. 244; Wert, pp. 357–62.

268 Lee had been a member of the board of visitors of the school in 1865–1870 when he was president of Washington College in nearby Lexington, Virginia. He also had sent two daughters to the school for their educations. Wert, p. 368 for recommendation.

269 Wert, pp. 368–69.

270 Wert, pp. 371–72.

271 Wert, p. 370.

272 Peterson, p. 353.

273 *Antique Trader*, December 27, 2006, p1, p. 15 (online auction site http://americana.heritageauctions.com/common/view_item.php?Sale_No=642&Lot_No=25448&type=)

274 Laurel Hill website http://www.freestateofpatrick.com/Laurelhill.

275 * Golden, Christopher, Bissette, Stephen, Sniegoski, Thomas E., *The Monster Book*, Simon & Schuster, 2000, ISBN 0-671-04259-9, p. 278.

276 IMDb. http://www.imdb.com/name/nm0298812/

277 Adams, Richard, *Traveller: A Novel*, Alfred A. Knopf, 1988, ISBN 0-440-20493-3.

278 Skimin, Robert, *Gray Victory*, St. Martin's Press, 1988, ISBN 0-312-01374-4.

279 Turtledove, Harry, *How Few Remain, Volume 1*, Random House, Inc., 1998, ISBN 0-345-40614-1, p. 45.

280 https://soundcloud.com/arborea/when-i-was-on-horseback

281 https://archive.org/stream/llfecampaignsotm00mccl#page/n6/mode/1up

282 https://books.google.com/books?id=toon6U-vAWIC

283 //www.worldcat.org/oclc/26692400

284 http://www.freestateofpatrick.com/laurelhillteachersguide2.pdf

285 http://www.jebstuart.org/

286 https://www.findagrave.com/cgi-bin/fg.cgi?page=gr&GRid=986

287 http://encyclopediavirginia.org/Stuart_J_E_B_1833-1864

288 Eicher, pp. 554–55.

289 Heidler, pp. 2062–63.

290 Wittenberg, p. 116.

291 Wittenberg, p. 117.

292 Wittenberg, p. 119.

293 Grant, p. 702.

294 Wittenberg, pp. 119–25.

[295] Wittenberg, pp. 127–31.
[296] Wittenberg, p. 129.
[297] http://www.gutenberg.org/etext/4367
[298]

Article Sources and Contributors

The sources listed for each article provide more detailed licensing information including the copyright status, the copyright owner, and the license conditions.

Retreat from Gettysburg *Source:* https://en.wikipedia.org/w/index.php?oldid=729190753 *License:* Creative Commons Attribution-Share Alike 3.0 *Contributors:* CWenger, Chris the speller, ClueBot NG, Daniel kenneth, FDRMRZUSA, Hlj, Johnfrancisc, Jrcrin001, JustBerry, KConWiki, Kresock, Mieczkowski, Nihiltres, Revb2, Richard Keatinge, Ryuhaku, Scott Mingus, Stevewxr, Target for Today, Vieque, 14 anonymous edits 5

Battle of Fairfield *Source:* https://en.wikipedia.org/w/index.php?oldid=723441452 *License:* Creative Commons Attribution-Share Alike 3.0 *Contributors:* 8th Ohio Volunteers, BD2412, Display name 99, Hlj, Hmains, Johnfrancisc, Jrcrin001, Jrnold, JustAGal, Mugs2109, Patar knight, Pubdog, Rheo1905, RobotG, Sardanaphalus, Scott Mingus, Target for Today, The Frog, Tim!, Wild Wolf, 6 anonymous edits 21

Fight at Monterey Pass *Source:* https://en.wikipedia.org/w/index.php?oldid=693970347 *License:* Creative Commons Attribution-Share Alike 3.0 *Contributors:* 8th Ohio Volunteers, American Money, Arbogastlw, Bedford, Bruce.guthrie, Gh5149, Hlj, Hmains, Johnfrancisc, Jwillbur, Ken Gallager, Mugs2109, Muhranoff, Raining123, Rich Farmbrough, Scott Mingus, Target for Today, The Frog, Tim!, Timrollpickering, Wild Wolf, 1 anonymous edits 24

Battle of Williamsport *Source:* https://en.wikipedia.org/w/index.php?oldid=734318198 *License:* Creative Commons Attribution-Share Alike 3.0 *Contributors:* 578, Adamdaley, American Money, Brian0918, CWenger, ClueBot NG, Foofighter20x, Hlj, Hmains, Jllm06, Johnfrancisc, Jrnold, Klsdad2012, MK2, Mieczkowski, NightMarinara, Rheo1905, Rich Farmbrough, RobotG, Roy Al Blue, Sardanaphalus, Scott Mingus, Tim!, Wild Wolf, 9 anonymous edits 31

Battle of Boonsboro *Source:* https://en.wikipedia.org/w/index.php?oldid=725819771 *License:* Creative Commons Attribution-Share Alike 3.0 *Contributors:* 578, 8th Ohio Volunteers, Adair2324, Adamdaley, Alai, Andrwsc, Brian0918, Caerwine, CapedFrito, Foofighter20x, GeeJo, Hlj, Hmains, Jllm06, Johnfrancisc, Jrnold, Ken Gallager, Kirill Lokshin, MrChupon, RobotG, Roy Al Blue, Scott Mingus, Tim!, Vpuliva, Wild Wolf, Wwoods, 3 anonymous edits 33

Battle of Funkstown *Source:* https://en.wikipedia.org/w/index.php?oldid=725828209 *License:* Creative Commons Attribution-Share Alike 3.0 *Contributors:* 8th Ohio Volunteers, CapedFrito, Frietjes, Hmains, Jllm06, Johnfrancisc, Jrnold, North Shoreman, Tim!, Wild Wolf, 1 anonymous edits .. 35

Battle of Manassas Gap *Source:* https://en.wikipedia.org/w/index.php?oldid=726116941 *License:* Creative Commons Attribution-Share Alike 3.0 *Contributors:* 578, Alai, Anbu121, Arbogastlw, Brannon0918, Caerwine, CapedFrito, Cl.q.lee, ClueBot NG, D6, Foofighter20x, GeeJo, Hlj, Hmains, J.delanoy, Jllm06, Johnfrancisc, MK2, Magioladitis, Mild Bill Hiccup, Rheo1905, Roy Al Blue, Tim!, Wild Wolf, Woohookitty, 15 anonymous edits 39

Bristoe Campaign *Source:* https://en.wikipedia.org/w/index.php?oldid=733405748 *License:* Creative Commons Attribution-Share Alike 3.0 *Contributors:* American Money, Beaversd, Civil Engineer III, FDRMRZUSA, Formerusr-82, Good Olfactory, Graham1973, Hlj, Hmains, Johnfrancisc, Jrcrin001, Kitt1987, Lieutcoluseng, Lockesdonkey, Lostcatholic, Military mad, Mojo Hand, Nevik.flor, Nihiltres, Roy Al Blue, Ryuhaku, Saga City, Scott Mingus, Ss55goku, Stevietheman, Target for Today, Valetude, Widr, Wild Wolf, 8 anonymous edits 41

First Battle of Auburn *Source:* https://en.wikipedia.org/w/index.php?oldid=727022209 *License:* Creative Commons Attribution-Share Alike 3.0 *Contributors:* Alai, Andrei Marzan, Arbogastlw, Bakeysaur99, Chris the speller, Closedmouth, EvanDiBiase, Hlj, Hmains, Jrnold, LittleWink, MK2, Manassas~enwiki, ProudIrishAspie, Pubdog, Raymondwinn, Roy Al Blue, The Anomebot2, Tim!, Wild Wolf, 2 anonymous edits 46

Second Battle of Auburn *Source:* https://en.wikipedia.org/w/index.php?oldid=727025063 *License:* Creative Commons Attribution-Share Alike 3.0 *Contributors:* Alai, Arbogastlw, Bakeysaur99, Ginsuloft, Hlj, Hmains, Johnfrancisc, Jrnold, Kscheffler, MK2, No1lakkersfan, ProudIrishAspie, Pubdog, Roy Al Blue, Tassedethe, The Anomebot2, Tim!, Urellm, Valetude, Wavelength, Wild Wolf, 5 anonymous edits 50

Battle of Bristoe Station *Source:* https://en.wikipedia.org/w/index.php?oldid=733405362 *License:* Creative Commons Attribution-Share Alike 3.0 *Contributors:* Adriantighe, Alai, Andrwsc, Anotherclown, Arbogastlw, Beaversd, Bender235, Brad101AWB, Colonel Hessler, Frietjes, Garzo, Graham1973, Hlj, Hmains, J JMesserly, Jboulet98, Jllm06, Johnfrancisc, Jrnold, Kumioko (renamed), Lieutcoluseng, MK2, Mazzgo&Gladys, Mattbuse, Mojo Hand, Mojoworker, ProudIrishAspie, Rich Farmbrough, Rockenonboy, Roy Al Blue, Smallbones, The Anomebot2, Tim!, TomIzbick, Uncle Milty, Vcl2000, Wild Wolf, Willi-willi, 31 anonymous edits 54

Battle of Buckland Mills *Source:* https://en.wikipedia.org/w/index.php?oldid=693952104 *License:* Creative Commons Attribution-Share Alike 3.0 *Contributors:* Alai, Andrwsc, Arbogastlw, Colonies Chris, Hlj, Hmains, Johnfrancisc, Jrnold, Leosls, MK2, Rich Farmbrough, Roy Al Blue, The Anomebot2, Tim!, Wild Wolf, 1 anonymous edits 58

Second Battle of Rappahannock Station *Source:* https://en.wikipedia.org/w/index.php?oldid=728977858 *License:* Creative Commons Attribution-Share Alike 3.0 *Contributors:* 8th Ohio Volunteers, Arbogastlw, Berean Hunter, Bigweeboy, Bryan Derksen, ERcheck, Hlj, Hmains, Jllm06, Johnfrancisc, Jrnold, Nathanlarson32767, ProudIrishAspie, Roy Al Blue, Spacini, The Anomebot2, Theseeker4, Tim!, Wikipelli, Wild Wolf, 6 anonymous edits 59

Battle of Mine Run *Source:* https://en.wikipedia.org/w/index.php?oldid=734463272 *License:* Creative Commons Attribution-Share Alike 3.0 *Contributors:* AjGAMER10145, Arbogastlw, Berean Hunter, Cheeseskates, ClueBot NG, Dissident, FDRMRZUSA, Foofighter20x, Frietjes, Hlj, Hmains, Howcheng, Jeremy Bentham, Johnfrancisc, Jrnold, Kingwhick, Kitt1987, Kresock, Margo&Gladys, Mieczkowski, Morgan Riley, Roy Al Blue, Ryuhaku, S3000, Tawkerbot2, The Anomebot2, Tim!, Valetude, Wild Wolf, Wwoods, 14 anonymous edits 63

William H. French *Source:* https://en.wikipedia.org/w/index.php?oldid=720619229 *License:* Creative Commons Attribution-Share Alike 3.0 *Contributors:* Alaney2k, BOTijo, Bender235, BusterD, Clarityfiend, Coffeinfreak, CutOfTies, Davepape, Ejosse1, Hlj, Hmains, Jfrenchnd, Jwillbur, Kumioko (renamed), Liamkasbar, Looper5920, Mejkravitz, Monegasque, OberRanks, OccultZone, PBS-AWB, ProudIrishAspie, Rich Farmbrough, RobotG, Scott Mingus, Ser Amantio di Nicolao, Spacini, The Mystery Man, Thismightbezach, Woohookitty, 10 anonymous edits 67

John D. Imboden *Source:* https://en.wikipedia.org/w/index.php?oldid=721197253 *License:* Creative Commons Attribution-Share Alike 3.0 *Contributors:* 1ForTheMoney, Arbogastlw, BusterD, Cenantua, ClueBot NG, Collect, CommonsDelinker, D6, Darth Jadus, Davehi1, Deflective, Donaldecoho, Donner60, Dubyavee, FangzofBlood, Hlj, Hmains, Kihein, Kingwhick, Kresock, Kumioko (renamed), Kwamikagami, Lekoren, Nimmo27, ProudIrishAspie, Rjwilmsi, Rklear, RobotG, Rockenonboy, Ryanlintelman, S2grand, Scott Mingus, Ser Amantio di Nicolao, Spacini, Swvalaw, Taterian, The Frog, Vaoverland, 17 anonymous edits 72

William E. Jones *Source:* https://en.wikipedia.org/w/index.php?oldid=729042020 *License:* Creative Commons Attribution-Share Alike 3.0 *Contributors:* 1ForTheMoney, 8th Ohio Volunteers, All Hallow's Wrath, Berean Hunter, BrownHairedGirl, Cincinnati47, ClueBot NG, CommonsDelinker, Corlier, Darth Jadus, Deb, Donner60, Drmies, Ejosse1, GELongstreet, HenryLi, Hlj, Hmains, I dream of horses, Joshmaul, Kingwhick, Klemen Kocjancic, Kresock, Kumioko (renamed), Liamkasbar, Michael Devore, Mickey Featherstone, Mogism, MountainRad, ProudIrishAspie, Pubdog, Remuel, Rich Farmbrough, Rklear, Rlevse, RobotG, Rockenonboy, Scott Mingus, StJackson, Tedernst, TennRebel19, The Frog, The wub, Touisiau, Woohookitty, Xiong Chiamiov, Zafiroblue05, Zawed, 28 anonymous edits 78

Hugh Judson Kilpatrick *Source:* https://en.wikipedia.org/w/index.php?oldid=714287856 *License:* Creative Commons Attribution-Share Alike 3.0 *Contributors:* 8th Ohio Volunteers, Alansohn, Aldis90, All Hallow's Wrath, Animalparty, Antandrus, BatteauX, Battousai, Berean Hunter, BlackBaron, Bob Burkhardt, Brianyoumans, CWenger, CanisRufus, Captain panda, Citation bot 1, Davepape, Donner60, Gaius Cornelius, HOT L Baltimore, Hlj, Hmains, JamesBWatson, Jcw69, JustAGal, Kingwhick, Kumioko (renamed), Looper5920, MrBoZ2846, Melromero, Merrikatt, Morgan Riley, Mstuczynski, NCHistoryProject, Nimetapoeg, Polylerus, Ponyo, ProudIrishAspie, Quale, R'n'B, Rich Farmbrough, RobDuch, RobotG, Ryuhaku, S2grand, Scewing, Scott Mingus, Searate1999, SimonP, Spacini, Steelerscanes1, Steven Kevil, Tech77, Theroadislong, Thismightbezach, Threeafterthree, TomIzbick, Trappist the monk, Tuckerresearch, Vanished user azby388723i8jfjh32, VoABot II, 44 anonymous edits 83

John Sedgwick *Source:* https://en.wikipedia.org/w/index.php?oldid=734313436 *License:* Creative Commons Attribution-Share Alike 3.0 *Contributors:* Ahodges7, Alansohn, AlistairMcMillan, Andrew Gray, Antonio Lopez, BCV, Bacchus77, Bantman, Bender235, Blueyoshi321, BohicaTwentyTwo, Breffni Whelan, Brian0918, BrownHairedGirl, BusterD, BuzyBody, CWenger, Chris the speller, ClueBot NG, Cuprum17, D6, DavidKVT, De Forest, Discospinster, DisillusionedBitterAndKnackered, Display name 99, Drmies, Effajay, Ejosse1, Elainewiener, Epbr123, ErrantX, EurekaLott, FatherKuroi, Flyer22 Reborn, Fred Bauder, Gaius Cornelius, Glacialsurge, Good Olfactory, Gothica36, Gwydion, HandsomeFella, Hendon, Herrick~enwiki, Hlj, Hmains, Hobbamock, Illegitimate Barrister, Isaac Rabinovitch, Jan Arkesteijn, Johnpacklambert, Joshmaul, Jwillbur, Kalaong, Kalki, Katieh5584, Kingwhick, Kirk!, Kumioko (renamed), Lady Rochford, Lightmouse, Livajo, Looper5920, LtNOVA, MK2, Marianocecenski, Markvs88, Materialscientist, McCart42, Mdw0, Michael David, Mickey Featherstone, Mieczkowski, Mike Selinker, Monegasque, Napa, Nehrams2020, Norm mit, OccultZone, Peter2212, Petersam, Pkino, ProudIrishAspie, Pubdog, Quadell, Rich Farmbrough, RobotG, Ryuhaku, Sander.v.Ginkel, Sbmeirow, Scewing, Scott Mingus, Seattlehawk94, SimonP, Spacini, Suisui, Ta bu shi da yu, The Frog, The Mystery Man, The wub, Thetalkinghands, Valetude, Varano, Weee96, Wwoods, ‏ציונימקרדי‎, 121 anonymous edits 92

J. E. B. Stuart *Source:* https://en.wikipedia.org/w/index.php?oldid=729003280 *License:* Creative Commons Attribution-Share Alike 3.0 *Contributors:* 248Garland, Accurizer, Alansohn, All Hallow's Wrath, Anotherclown, Arethuca v, Axcrc, BDD, Bellerophon5685, Bender235, Berean Hunter, Beyond My Ken, Broberds, BusterD, CWenger, Cantabrigidian, Captain-n00dle, Cherkash, Chowbok, Chris the speller, Cl22NazeeriA, Clarityfiend, ClueBot NG, Colsfan, CommonsDelinker, Connormah, Courcelles, CutOfTies, DVdm, DemocraticLuntz, Discospinster, Dombrownphan, Donner60, Dorkrock, Easyid, Epicgenius, FaTaLxFaKi, Fdewaele, Foofbun, Fox2k11, Froid, GELongstreet, Gaarmyvet, GabeHanafin, GcSwRhIc, Gchoate17, Gigemag76, Glacialfox, Grblomerth, Gråbergs Gråa Sång, GusF, Gypsy18, HennessyC, Hlj, Howcheng, Hushpuckena, Ibadibam, Illegitimate Barrister, Jack Breeze, Jay

Image Sources, Licenses and Contributors

The sources listed for each image provide more detailed licensing information including the copyright status, the copyright owner, and the license conditions.

Figure 1 *Source:* https://en.wikipedia.org/w/index.php?title=File:Meade_and_Lee.jpg *License:* Copyrighted free use *Contributors:* BrokenSphere, Goldfishbutt, Rheo1905∼commonswiki, 1 anonymous edits 6
Figure 2 *Source:* https://en.wikipedia.org/w/index.php?title=File:Gettysburg_Campaign_Retreat.png *License:* Creative Commons Attribution 3.0 *Contributors:* Drawn by Hal Jespersen in Adobe Illustrator CS5 9
Figure 3 *Source:* https://en.wikipedia.org/w/index.php?title=File:Monterey_Pass.png *License:* Creative Commons Attribution 3.0 *Contributors:* Hal Jespersen 10
Figure 4 *Source:* https://en.wikipedia.org/w/index.php?title=File:Meade_crossing_Antietam_Edwin_Forbes.jpg *License:* Public Domain *Contributors:* Forbes, Edwin, 1839-1895, artist. Illus. in: Frank Leslie's illustrated newspaper, v. 16, no. 409 (1863 Aug. 1), p. 304. 14
Figure 5 *Source:* https://en.wikipedia.org/w/index.php?title=File:Lee_retreat_earthworks_Edwin_Forbes.jpg *License:* Public Domain *Contributors:* Forbes, Edwin, 1839-1895, artist 15
Figure 6 *Source:* https://en.wikipedia.org/w/index.php?title=File:Lee's_Retreat_Edwin_Forbes.jpg *License:* Public Domain *Contributors:* Forbes, Edwin, 1839-1895, artist 17
Image *Source:* https://en.wikipedia.org/w/index.php?title=File:US_flag_34_stars.svg *License:* Public Domain *Contributors:* Abjiklam, Benzoyl, Cycn, Homo lupus, Illegitimate Barrister, Jacobolus, SiBr4, Wikiborg, Zscout370, 3 anonymous edits 21
Image *Source:* https://en.wikipedia.org/w/index.php?title=File:Second_national_flag_of_the_Confederate_States_of_America.svg *Contributors:* - 21
Figure 7 *Source:* https://en.wikipedia.org/w/index.php?title=File:Judson_Kilpatrick.jpg *License:* Public Domain *Contributors:* Hlj, Monkeybait, Sfan00 IMG 26
Figure 8 *Source:* https://en.wikipedia.org/w/index.php?title=File:William_Edmondson_Jones.jpg *License:* Public Domain *Contributors:* Magog the Ogre, OgreBot 2, Reguyla 27
Figure 9 *Source:* https://en.wikipedia.org/w/index.php?title=File:Monterey_Pass.png *License:* Creative Commons Attribution 3.0 *Contributors:* Hal Jespersen 30
Image *Source:* https://en.wikipedia.org/w/index.php?title=File:Commons-logo.svg *License:* logo *Contributors:* Anomie, Callanecc, RHaworth 30
Image *Source:* https://en.wikipedia.org/w/index.php?title=File:The_pursuit_of_Gen._Lee's_rebel_army,_July_10,_1863.png *License:* Public Domain *Contributors:* File Upload Bot (Magnus Manske), Kelly, Taterian 31
Image *Source:* https://en.wikipedia.org/w/index.php?title=File:US_flag_35_stars.svg *License:* Public Domain *Contributors:* Abjiklam, Benzoyl, Cycn, Homo lupus, Illegitimate Barrister, Jacobolus, SiBr4, Zscout370, 1 anonymous edits 31
Figure 10 *Source:* https://en.wikipedia.org/w/index.php?title=File:Gettysburg_Campaign_Retreat.png *License:* Creative Commons Attribution 3.0 *Contributors:* Drawn by Hal Jespersen in Adobe Illustrator CS5 32
Figure 11 *Source:* https://en.wikipedia.org/w/index.php?title=File:Gettysburg_Campaign_Retreat.png *License:* Creative Commons Attribution 3.0 *Contributors:* Drawn by Hal Jespersen in Adobe Illustrator CS5 34
Figure 12 *Source:* https://en.wikipedia.org/w/index.php?title=File:Gettysburg_Campaign_Retreat.png *License:* Creative Commons Attribution 3.0 *Contributors:* Drawn by Hal Jespersen in Adobe Illustrator CS5 36
Figure 13 *Source:* https://en.wikipedia.org/w/index.php?title=File:Bristoe_Campaign.png *License:* Creative Commons Attribution 3.0 *Contributors:* Hal Jespersen at en.wikipedia 43
Figure 14 *Source:* https://en.wikipedia.org/w/index.php?title=File:Bristoe_Campaign.png *License:* Creative Commons Attribution 3.0 *Contributors:* Hal Jespersen at en.wikipedia 47
Figure 15 *Source:* https://en.wikipedia.org/w/index.php?title=File:Bristoe_Campaign.png *License:* Creative Commons Attribution 3.0 *Contributors:* Hal Jespersen at en.wikipedia 51
Figure 16 *Source:* https://en.wikipedia.org/w/index.php?title=File:Bristoe_Campaign.png *License:* Creative Commons Attribution 3.0 *Contributors:* Hal Jespersen at en.wikipedia 55
Figure 17 *Source:* https://en.wikipedia.org/w/index.php?title=File:BATTLE_OF_BRISTOW_STATION,_PRINCE_WILLIAM_COUNTY.JPG *License:* Creative Commons Attribution-Sharealike 3.0 *Contributors:* User:KLOTZ 56
Image *Source:* https://en.wikipedia.org/w/index.php?title=File:Harper's_Weekly_-_Battle_of_Mine_Run_-_Gen_Warren's_Troops_Attacking.jpg *License:* Public Domain *Contributors:* William Waud (original sketch) 63
Figure 18 *Source:* https://en.wikipedia.org/w/index.php?title=File:Mine_Run_Campaign.png *License:* Creative Commons Attribution 3.0 *Contributors:* Hal Jespersen 64
Figure 19 *Source:* https://en.wikipedia.org/w/index.php?title=File:Harper's_Weekly_-_Scene_at_Germanna_Ford.jpg *License:* Public Domain *Contributors:* William Waud (original sketch) 64
Image *Source:* https://en.wikipedia.org/w/index.php?title=File:William_H._French_-_Brady-Handy.jpg *License:* Public Domain *Contributors:* BrokenSphere, Davepape, Romary 67
Image *Source:* https://en.wikipedia.org/w/index.php?title=File:Union_army_maj_gen_rank_insignia.jpg *License:* Public Domain *Contributors:* US-O7_insignia.svg: Ipankonin derivative work: Hoodinski (talk) 67
Figure 20 *Source:* https://en.wikipedia.org/w/index.php?title=File:Potomac_Staff.jpg *License:* Public Domain *Contributors:* Animalparty, Bob Burkhardt, BotMultichill, BrokenSphere, Marv1N, Maxrossomachin, OgreBot 2, SalomonCeb, 1 anonymous edits 70
Figure 21 *Source:* https://en.wikipedia.org/w/index.php?title=File:French_and_Staff.jpg *License:* Public Domain *Contributors:* Civil War glass negative collection (Library of Congress). 70
Image *Source:* https://en.wikipedia.org/w/index.php?title=File:PD-icon.svg *License:* Public Domain *Contributors:* Alex.muller, Anomie, Anonymous Dissident, CBM, MBisanz, PBS, Quadell, Rocket000, Strangerer, Timotheus Canens, 1 anonymous edits 71
Image *Source:* https://en.wikipedia.org/w/index.php?title=File:John_D._Imboden.jpg *License:* Public Domain *Contributors:* Brady National Photographic Art Gallery 72
Image *Source:* https://en.wikipedia.org/w/index.php?title=File:Confederate_States_of_America_General.png *License:* Public Domain *Contributors:* User:goran_tek-en 72
Figure 22 *Source:* https://en.wikipedia.org/w/index.php?title=File:Gen._J.D._Imboden,_C.S.A._-_NARA_-_529238.jpg *License:* Public Domain *Contributors:* AdamBMorgan, Michael Barera 73
Figure 23 *Source:* https://en.wikipedia.org/w/index.php?title=File:Imboden's_movements.png *License:* Creative Commons Attribution-Sharealike 2.5 *Contributors:* & Karl Musser (original map) / en:User:Donaldecoho (changes) 75
Image *Source:* https://en.wikipedia.org/w/index.php?title=File:US_flag_31_stars.svg *License:* Public Domain *Contributors:* User:Jacobolus 78
Image *Source:* https://en.wikipedia.org/w/index.php?title=File:Flag_of_the_United_States_Army.svg *License:* Public Domain *Contributors:* United States Army 78
Image *Source:* https://en.wikipedia.org/w/index.php?title=File:Battle_flag_of_the_US_Confederacy.svg *Contributors:* - 78
Image *Source:* https://en.wikipedia.org/w/index.php?title=File:Union_army_1st_lt_rank_insignia.jpg *License:* Creative Commons Attribution-Sharealike 3.0 *Contributors:* Hoodinski 78
Image *Source:* https://en.wikipedia.org/w/index.php?title=File:Flag_of_Virginia_(1861).svg *License:* Public Domain *Contributors:* User:Ali Zifan 78
Figure 24 *Source:* https://en.wikipedia.org/w/index.php?title=File:WilliamEJones.jpg *License:* Public Domain *Contributors:* Berean Hunter .. 80
Image *Source:* https://en.wikipedia.org/w/index.php?title=File:Gen._Judson_Kilpatrick_-_NARA_-_528309-crop.jpg *License:* Public Domain *Contributors:* Scewing 83
Figure 25 *Source:* https://en.wikipedia.org/w/index.php?title=File:Hugh_Judson_Kilpatrick_-_Chancellorsville_Campaign.jpg *License:* Public Domain *Contributors:* Chowbok, Davepape, Man vyi, Scewing, Thib Phil, WFinch 85
Figure 26 *Source:* https://en.wikipedia.org/w/index.php?title=File:HughJudsonKilpatrick.jpg *License:* Public Domain *Contributors:* Berean Hunter, Scewing 86
Figure 27 *Source:* https://en.wikipedia.org/w/index.php?title=File:Hugh_Judson_Kilpatrick_and_3d_Division_staff.jpg *License:* Public Domain *Contributors:* BoringHistoryGuy, Davepape, Scewing 87
Image *Source:* https://en.wikipedia.org/w/index.php?title=File:John_Sedgwick.png *License:* Public Domain *Contributors:* File Upload Bot (Magnus Manske), Giggy, OgreBot 2, Quadell, Sfan00 IMG 92
Image *Source:* https://en.wikipedia.org/w/index.php?title=File:John_Sedgwick_signature.svg *License:* Public Domain *Contributors:* John Sedgwick Created in vector format by Scewing 92

License

Index